Overthinking

Toxic Thoughts That Can Destroy Your Relationship

(Master Your Mind by Increasing Your Self-esteem, Eliminating Anxiety and Clutter)

Robert Creed

Published By **Bella Frost**

Robert Creed

All Rights Reserved

Overthinking: Toxic Thoughts That Can Destroy Your Relationship (Master Your Mind by Increasing Your Self-esteem, Eliminating Anxiety and Clutter)

ISBN 978-1-7773679-2-3

No part of this guidebook shall be reproduced in any form without permission in writing from the publisher except in the case of brief quotations embodied in critical articles or reviews.

Legal & Disclaimer

The information contained in this book is not designed to replace or take the place of any form of medicine or professional medical advice. The information in this book has been provided for educational & entertainment purposes only.

The information contained in this book has been compiled from sources deemed reliable, and it is accurate to the best of the Author's knowledge; however, the Author cannot guarantee its accuracy and validity and cannot be held liable for any errors or omissions. Changes are periodically made to this book. You must consult your doctor or get professional medical advice before using any of the suggested remedies, techniques, or information in this book.

Upon using the information contained in this book, you agree to hold harmless the Author from and against any damages, costs, and expenses, including any legal fees potentially resulting from the application of any of the information provided by this guide. This disclaimer applies to any damages or injury caused by the use and application, whether directly or indirectly, of any advice or information presented, whether for breach of contract, tort, negligence, personal injury, criminal intent, or under any other cause of action.

You agree to accept all risks of using the information presented inside this book. You need to consult a professional medical practitioner in order to ensure you are both able and healthy enough to participate in this program.

Table Of Contents

Chapter 1: The Benefits Of Sacrificing Happiness 1

Chapter 2: The Joys Of Life And Avoiding Thinking 6

Chapter 3: How To Determine The Lists Of Opposition 13

Chapter 4: The Benefits Of Giving Up 26

Chapter 5: Strategies For Giving Up 30

Chapter 6: Dealing With Pain And Misfortune 34

Chapter 7: Breaking Dangerous Links 49

Chapter 8: The Giving Up Of Any Presence To Limit Thoughts 73

Chapter 9: Accepting The Risk As Well As The Adaptability 87

Chapter 10: A Life That Is Purpose-Driven 99

Chapter 11: Anxiety Stress, Negative Idea 111

Chapter 12: Ending The Conflict And Welcoming Inspiration 123

Chapter 13: Develop A Strategy For Your Day 144

Chapter 14: Keep Going With The Moderate Lifestyle 157

Chapter 15: Terribly Connections 171

Chapter 1: The Benefits Of Sacrificing Happiness

Why would it be a good idea to look at the possibility of giving often?

Since, dear reader, this is the main ingredient in satisfaction and self-awareness. Holding on to the past and burying regrets and arguing over irrelevant issues mainly creates a feeling of heaviness and hinder our growth.

The act of letting go opens doors to fresh opportunities, new experiences and a profound sensation of tranquility. You must be mentally tough to confront your doubts as well as admit the mistakes you made, and then part of things or people that aren't going to contribute again to the success of your business. It is certainly not an indication of weakening.

Contentment, happiness and the growth of our own self-confidence are achievable if we don't do not give up. This is a way to reveal our true selves flexibility, self-adjustment, and stronger presence.

Growth and achievement are inextricably connected with the decision to quit.

"Sense of Connection": Studying the neuroscience of connections within the brain

The human fundamental trait of connecting has deeply psychological underpinnings. People tend to build lasting, strong bonds with places, people as well as objects.

The connections we make are a result of early interactions especially during our early period, where we form connections to our professions. These bonds, also referred to by the name of connection type, can have an effect on our emotional control and the future structure of our relationships.

The first step in comprehending the reasons we keep certain people, things or notions and why it is difficult to let go of them is to comprehend the study of brain connections.

Clinicians have identified a range of kinds of relationship types, like security, reluctance, and avoidant.

They have an effect on how we perceive, our actions and our attitudes when we are when we are in a cooperative or relational setting.

Resources, convictions, and associations: the various types of associations

It is possible to connect in numerous areas of our lives. It does not only refer to social connections.

The associations that are directly tied to our relationship to family members, companions as well as colleagues and friends typically have the strongest. Connectivity, which is good or bad, influence our feelings of safety, trust as well as closeness.

Assemblies with Possession

The sentiments of awe that beautiful objects can invoke are either triggered through objects of material or could be result of our real world. There is a good chance that we're not in any way the only people who are that are settling us.

Conviction Association

Additionally, we could be deeply embedded in our beliefs regarding religious issues, government, or even reasoning. This could cause us to be unable to speak with a neutral voice and remain conscious of ourselves. The thoughts and beliefs of people are closely linked.

Connectivity to previous Trades

The process of reviewing both positive and negative past events can help build bonds. If we're sucked into regret or the achievements that have occurred in the past, it's likely to be difficult as regards our ability in pursuing our goals.

In recollecting these connections it is possible to begin the process that involves getting rid of things which isn't helping us in the long run. Each of these relationships have the potential to affect the course of our lives in a significant way. It is crucial to understand these diverse aspects of organizations before deciding to give up.

The vast possibilities of Human Connection

Our thoughts, feelings as well as ways of being greatly influenced by the connections we make that can be both simple as well as exacerbate our anxiety. We are influenced by connections in a variety of ways. For instance:

Positive Influence

Solid relationships give us a feelings of safety as well as love and encouragement that allow us to improve and cherish the things in our lives.

Negative impact

Intimate relationships may hinder the self-awareness and happiness of a person by creating inner turmoil, dependency, and sometimes conflicts.

Chapter 2: The Joys Of Life And Avoiding Thinking

What's the problem with over thinking?

In today's hectic environment It's easy to get overwhelmed by the stress of thinking too much.

We are constantly flooded with ideas worry, fears and fears could prevent us from fully enjoying our lives.

Rumination, a different term for excessive thinking, is a typical mental habit that is characterized by a lot of and repeated pondering that are usually focused on one particular problem such as a situation, idea, or even a particular event.

Over and over again examining various aspects of an area, sometimes overly-focused--and often failing to come up with the most appropriate answer or an objective conclusion can be a sign of overthinking.

The most common examples of excessive analysis include:

A. Dozing off the past

B. worry about the future.

C. always examining the current.

These are the signs that indicate overthinking:

Monotonous Thoughts: People who are overthinkers tend to think for hours because they are constantly re-visiting the same issues, questions or even thoughts.

The problem is that people who analyze situations too much will nearly all the time be overwhelmed by their anxiety about making an wrong choice and conducting extensive investigation to come up with a straightforward choice.

Example of a Pessimistic Concept People who are obsessed with certain things are more likely to view things in a negative or horribly and imagine the worst case scenario.

A crucial investment channel is overanalyzing issues at the end of the tunnel will consume lots of energy and time that can affect efficiency and the enjoyment of the present.

The body and mind: A prolonged focus on analysis may cause stress, anxiety and in the case of a surprise, major complaints, such as

headaches,

Sleeplessness and

exhaustion.

The Present is not the only thing that matters People who be overthinking things sometimes are unable to truly engage with situation and people they're currently having to deal with.

The development of protocols that monitor and limit overthinking is crucial to ensure mental wellbeing and personal growth.

Though a degree of precise analytical thinking is required to be able to think critically and provide guidance however, excessive analysis can cause danger when it is detrimental to day-today function and causes problems or makes one feel unsatisfied or unproductive.

Strategies to avoid over-analyzing while valuing the moment and the place to truly take in the pleasures of life.

1. The thoughts and concerns

Regularly scheduled care will help you build a stronger confidence in your thoughts and feelings, as well as an appreciation of the beauty of your present.

Since contemplation and care allow us to focus our attention on the present and to acknowledge thoughts, without judging them They are effective methods to overcome the habit of overthinking.

2. Find out the habits of overthinking

Overthinking is a process that requires a thorough understanding of your habits. After you've pinpointed the circumstances such as events or situations which cause you stress, try practicing strategies to relax your mind whenever you notice yourself analyzing too much.

3. Set time Cutoffs to allow for merely making the decision

Set the deadlines that you must meet for self-direction. Focusing on making a choice within a predetermined timeframe helps you to break free from the mental traps of overanalyzing and decrease the amount of time you spend ruminating.

Most of the time, anxiety can lead to excessive thinking.

4. Engage in Stream Athletics

Participate in activities, sports or activities suitable for your present circumstance and offer your with an edge. As these types of activities put you in a flow that is focussed and focused and can assist you to not overthink.

5. Make sure you are aware of your the self-care you do

Healthy bodies can help to maintain a positive mind. Taking proper care of your physical as well as mental wellbeing is vital for avoiding thinking too much. You should get adequate time to sleep, adhere to a healthy eating plan, and get active often.

6. Expressing gratitude

Start a gratitude journal or taking a moment each morning to look back on the positive things about your life could help change your mindset from being apathetic about issues to embracing the little delights that life has to offer.

7. Connect with the natural world

Being outdoors in nature or taking a journey or simply relaxing in an area for recreation can assist you in letting go of analyzing everything and allow you to appreciate all what is good in the world.

8. Confine Data Social Gathering

Today, information is everywhere. Be selective with your media and entertainment consumption since these media frequently trigger excessive thinking on the world or deep analysis.

9. Get Help

A conversation with a trusted person or a professional about your concerns and thoughts could, in a way give you some perspective, and allow you stop analyzing too much.

Incorporating these strategies in your routines and learning how to decrease anxiety, be more in tune with the moment and be more open to the many experiences the world has to give you.

Remember that changing requires the use of some self-control in your efforts to get rid of the burden of overthinking and discover your own unique capacity to maximize the enjoyment the world around you. Avoiding overthinking things and focusing on the small things are a constant process.

Chapter 3: How To Determine The Lists Of Opposition

Watching while you're clenching

It's crucial to identify that you're hanging on prior to you can begin the process of let go.

As connections tend to be far beyond our consciousness, it might not be always possible.

What you must be able to see as you hold on to the rope:

First step in letting the past go is taking the moment to look at what's going through your head. It could be thoughts of the person you are thinking about or a grudge, fantasies, or conviction or belief system.

Effects of Clutching: It could be a sign of stress, pressure, or even, in some cases, discomfort. Sometimes, our bodies display the blockage our bodies are suffering from.

Dark Thoughts: Keeping a close eye on the past or worrying about the future can cause you to be unable to let go. It's a sign that you are connected if your thoughts continue to revert back to the same person or situation.

Discord in Relationships: Constant disputes, mainly over similar topics, may be a sign the possibility that you or your close family member are clinging to things that need to be let go.

Standard operations, Profound and the Social Indicators of Opposition

The desire to never give up can be seen in our attitudes and actions on a regular on a regular. The most common tips to be aware of include:

Fear is among the strength of associations. The reason for this is usually an anxiety about the unknown or the fear of the loss of something that is important.

Rage and Hatred

The resentment that is buried in feelings Unresolved conflicts, unfinished business, or the old wounds that have accumulated can cause anger and displeasure.

Anxiety

Unease and anxiety in particular about results which we are not able to control, could suggest a relationship.

Stalling

Refusing to make decisions or engage in actions that let you continue may suggest a desire to end relations.

Secluded

If you're finding it hard to get along with people, or even accept assistance from them this could indicate that you're committing to the wrong behavior.

Personal Accounts and Contextual Research

In order to bring the concepts of surrender and resistance more into the real world We will look at the personal experiences of people who have experienced it and confirm analyses of contexts that focus on the difficulties people faced in securing their possessions and taking actions when they learned to give up.

Sarah's Battle with a Poisonous Fellowship

The principal contextual inquiry will examine Sarah's unique preuve of her relationship to this harmful friendship as well as her actions in order to free herself from the negative effects of it.

The 25-year-old Sarah has a job in promotion and has been an ardent person who's supported her faithful lover Lisa throughout many difficulties.

In time, Sarah began to see the fact that her love for Lisa had a negative influence on her overall well-being.

The pivotal moment occurred at the point that Lisa began to exercise greater control and deterrence. She would continuously be critical of Sarah's appearance, achievements, and--surprisingly--friends that she made.

Sarah was feeling even more isolated and uncomfortable as a result of her affinities with Lisa and Lisa, who tied her to this unwholesome relationship.

Sarah was aware that something had to be changed after placing her faith in a close friend, Emily, who assisted her to identify the weaknesses within her relationships with Lisa and helped her think about the detrimental impact that it had on her life. It was clear for Sarah that something needed to be done about it.

Engaging in a candid discussion with Lisa about her goals in their relationship, after everything, it became clear that Lisa's reluctance to discuss the matter was Sarah's best-known act in addition to setting limits and requesting to be treated with respect.

Sarah was able to reduce her hours with Lisa and a lot more time with friends who gave her confidence, after she realized that she needed to get over Lisa's influence.

Then she started engaging in activities that helped increase her self-confidence. Sarah was eventually treated to heal her severe injury and enhance her social abilities.

In the perfect moment Sarah's life began to get better; she felt at peace, grew stronger to her family, and she was able to enjoy a resurgence of her wealth.

Her story serves an excellent example of why it's so important to identify poisonous connections and to establish the stopping points, collect assistance, and take the final decision to stop harmful effects in order to lead an enjoyable, healthier living.

The journey of Forgiveness

John's story will help explain how he was able to forgive and accepting past mistakes, while also revealing the implications for his psychological well-being.

John was a forty-year old executive, had been concerned about a significant issue for quite a while that was a well-established anger towards his father, who was the one to say a final goodbye to him even though his son was still a small teenager. John's career, status in society and overall prosperity were totally influenced by the disrespectful behavior of his father.

A significant amount of period, John was angry and violent due to his father's absence. The negative feelings he felt had an impact on his personal existence, which made it tough to establish connections and earn the trust of others.

The inability of his to gain control of his emotions meant that his connections were marred by envy and a lack of confidence, but his passion remained.

However, the situation began to shift after John was seeking treatment for his atypical concerns. At first the situation appeared unimaginable that a specialist would advise him to think about the possibility of cleaning up his father's image however, the expert stated that his goal was to release him from any responsibility that dad's behavior have brought on him.

John was able to go through an incredible process of reconciliation which required a lot of thought and a keen eye. He finally understood that holding his anger in his hands could cause it to hurt, and he decided to put aside his anger.

He finally found an avenue of transportation near to his house and a sense of inner peace he'd never experienced before.

John's account demonstrates that becoming content and mindful requires letting go of the deeply ingrained negative feelings.

This is in addition to the crucial positive impact of being easy-going an impact on the psychological wellbeing of people. After his recovery and a new start, John had the option to form new connections to make progress as well as find peace and harmony within his community.

Initial Private Account: Jennifer's Deviation from Balance

The main subject in this tale is Jennifer's decision to let go of possessions to pursue happiness with a little discipline.

Jennifer who was 32 years old and a visually-oriented craftsperson, recognized that she was following her experience of being trapped in a sea of possessions. She was always looking for new products. has left her to be unsatisfied and disengaged while her world was filled with items that did not make much distinction.

Following the incident of seeing a documentary about being a poor person, Jennifer began to ask the reason she needed material items in her daily routine.

The woman also realized the fact that her erratic environmental conditions resulted from her brain's confusion that prevented her from finding the joy that was evident. The path to balance began at this point.

Jennifer was out for her quest to find the balance. Her meticulous examination of everything in every room, making sure to keep only those things that gave real value to her existence. She discarded the unnecessary and experienced a sense of being transported.

Beyond her natural circumstances Jennifer's changes were due to a change in her needs She began to appreciate experiences over possessions and material things as she found joy with the gathering of beloved people as opposed to collection of money and also began to concentrate on her personal life, and gave the opportunity to pursue side-interests as well as personal development.

Jennifer's quiet way of living allowed her to experience the beauty of solitude and reduced her dependence on possessions and, consequently, encouraged her to attain joy. Her joy was living in a way that was fair and valued the importance of life's non-material gifts.

Since Jennifer took the choice to let go of her unwanted commercialization to be able to enjoy the ease of achieving dreams Jennifer's story illustrates how much control is possible when making changes to one's way of life.

The Individual Account II: The Transformation of Engraving Through Evolving Thoughts

The story of Engraving will show the way that adopting an improved attitude and abandoning the idea of contracting helped him achieve the highest level of personal as well as professional achievement.

The tale of Engraving serves as an example of the raging influence that a person's beliefs can affect the flow of instances, through as well as expertly.

In the past, when Engraving was younger, Engraving retained a certain perspective in accepting his capabilities as well as knowledge were inherent and irrevocable. The perspective he held stifled his true potential, and prevented his from progressing farther.

The second crucial event occurred after engraving was able to meet a mentor who explained to him the notion of the perspective of improvement. He was urged to recognize that capabilities and capabilities can be developed from hard work and a sense of obligation and commitment, he made the option of letting go of the limiting beliefs.

Engrave began to set out powerful goals, and advancing beyond his usual safe zone thanks to his new outlook which allowed him to adapt and overcome challenges with a degree of flexibility.

He sought out additional education and was looking for challenges at work, and embraced the failures as opportunities to improve and improve.

His professional life and his personal lives little by little, his life was transformed. Engraving took his work up to a new and took on tasks that frightened him in the past. The result was unquestionably.

In addition He outlined additional positive connections through fostering an environment where people are able to grow and strengthen the other.

Through adopting an improvement-oriented mindset instead of a correct one Engraving was able to reach his highest potential and demonstrate the incredible power of self-confidence and consistency. The case of Engraving shows how this kind of mindset shift can lead to success for the individual as well as to the professional.

These tales and the contextual explanations are a great summary of the ideas contained in the book. It will demonstrate to readers that giving up can be a challenge, but it is also is a path to satisfaction and personal growth.

Chapter 4: The Benefits Of Giving Up

Personal Independence and Health, as well as Emotional Health

Learning enough to quit is an essential step towards freedom and a healthy lifestyle close to the home.

If you can let go of those ties that were hindering you it is possible let go of the burden of your old and begin stepping into a promising future.

Localized Opportunities: You could get rid of the web that's been keeping your shackles by letting go. Maybe a huge burden is lifted off your shoulders, leading to an inner peace as well as opportunities nearer to home.

Reducing Stress: Connecting frequently creates tension and anxiety. Eliminating yourself from these bonds decreases stress and boosts the overall happiness of your life.

Better mental health A key aspect of mental well-being could involve giving up. This aids in the management of mental health issues such as anxiety or depression as well as excessively emotional issues, by decreasing an impulsive attitude and thinking.

The ability to cleanse

The power of forgiveness is transformative after one has given up. You can't just forgive people; you must also be able to let yourself forgive yourself. Being able to forgive can have an the ability to affect the quality of your life.

Building Relations

Pardoning may lead to more connections and restoration of damaged relations. The course focuses on understanding and surrendering.

Delivery close to your home

Removing anger, contempt or resentment releases your heart from the weight of their resentment. By committing yourself to self-giving it is possible to live your life in a calmer, more positive way.

Self-Compassion

It's possible to develop self-empathy through forgiveness. The practice acknowledges that mistakes will happen but that's okay. Self-forgiveness is the first step towards self-awareness, and acknowledging oneself.

Incorporating New Conceptual Outcomes in the Account

The best part about this cycle is having the opportunity to surrender and gain exciting new experiences as well as possibilities in your everyday routine. The process of letting go of the past creates an opportunity to embrace the future.

Fresh Partnerships: It's possible to open up your daily life for new and better relationships through the release of relationships that are toxic or ineffective.

Effective Development: Getting rid of rigid concepts and attachments to a certain work system can create new career opportunities as well as advancements.

Removing the outdated version of oneself is a important step in self-development and discovery of oneself. It is an opportunity to be the most perfect self-image you can be.

Experiential Learning and research: stepping out of your normal routine and embracing the change can help you become more open to ventures that you haven't thought of before.

There are many real and amazing advantages of giving up, and not only in the academic realm. This chapter will explore every aspect of getting these benefits into your life and making the process of giving up something that is a rewarding and rewarding experience.

Chapter 5: Strategies For Giving Up

Awareness and care

Developing consciousness and understanding is main step in the process of surrender.

If you follow these principles, you'll be able to better understand your relationships, and how they mean for you.

The discussion will focus on techniques for caring and contemplation to assist you in becoming more conscious of your feelings and thoughts and live your life fully in the moment. The process of recognizing links starts with increased consciousness.

The ability to perceive people in the most fundamental way

Being aware of your feelings and the way they affect the relationships you have with others is essential. It is our goal to determine whether it's possible to understand someone in depth and then how it relates to abandoning.

Maintaining a diary

A great way to be more aware of the person you truly are could be keeping a journal. Journals can provide you with valuable memories by helping you communicate your thoughts, feelings and preferences in communication.

Possible activities to give up Connectivity

It's not an abstract concept but something that can be taught and practiced.

This is the Particular Delivery. We'll talk about the method of providing substantial or similar securities. This is an intelligent approach for getting rid of objects that have become useless for the buyer.

The activities of appreciation: Being aware and having the awareness of your strengths could help you to give up more easily. The following article outlines a number of exercises for appreciation to help to shift your mindset.

Methods to Pardon: Forgiveness is about accepting forgiveness for others and yourself. To assist you in this incredible moment, we'll offer methods and exercises for forgiveness the other.

Cleaning and moderation In the event that you are attached to things that aren't yours, we'll give guidance on how you can get rid of clutter and maintain a healthy lifestyle and give you the opportunity to make your life better.

Requesting assistance from others

Quitting the habit can sometimes be daunting and lonely. The assistance of others may help you stay on track and provide support.

Connect with Steady Connections: We'll speak about the importance to surround yourself with people who are able to recognize when you need to quit and will be able to offer significant help.

Therapy and Counseling: Finding professional guidance from mentors and advisors can prove helpful, especially in the circumstances of deeply embedded relationships with family members and the traumas.

Being involved in care groups or groups of people with similar interest can create a safe place for members to talk about their personal experiences and receive help.

Chapter 6: Dealing With Pain And Misfortune

Solving this Misery of Misfortune

Unfortunate events are an inherent aspect of human existence.

Whatever catastrophe it is--a loved one quitting, a change in career losing the value of a property or simply a life adjustment to the ache of a mishap can be very challenging.

This article explains the process of dealing with the difficult experiences that come with bad luck. We provide the strategies, guidance and knowledge to help through the challenging period.

Embracing Adversity

One common reaction to poor luck is despair. It's an intricate and frequently intense mix of feelings that can include and sorrow, anger, sadness, or even support. The first step is to accept the suffering. stage in adjusting to pain of loss.

Elisabeth Kubler Ross, a psychologist has identified five stages of grief:

resistance,

outrage,

bartering,

Grief,

acknowledgment.

It's crucial to recognize that mourning isn't an unending process. You might experience them at times or in different sequences.

Distinctly unique Differences: Everybody uniquely experiences despair. People may decide to keep their feelings in check while others might be able to express their sadness on the streets. This is a personal process There's no one right method to express sadness about it.

Adaptable Techniques for Weeping

For overcoming the problem of being close to home of moping, you need to put in the effort, demonstrate empathy towards oneself and possess several strategies in difficult circumstances.

These survival techniques can help you overcome suffering:

Don't be a Brutus Affirming your grief is often a cause for the healing process to be slower. Let yourself feel the hurt, sadness, and anger. Accept the feelings, but without judging them.

Self-compassion: Allow yourself to have an opportunity to indulge in the difficult time. Losing a loved one or family member can be extremely stressful. Concentrate to your health by getting adequate sleep, eating your diet in a balanced way, and participating in pursuits that make you feel happy.

Review Your Feelings and Beliefs Discuss your feelings with someone who is a professional, friend or family member, or even someone you trust regarding your concerns and feelings. Talking about your issues could bring about a fantastic solution.

Honor and remember Make a thoughtful tribute to someone or an object that you lost. It could involve putting together the scrapbook of memories you cherish or planting a tree or having a memorial ceremony.

Ask for Help: rely on your network of support. Being able to find genuine compassion and an understanding listener from friends, family or even support groups can be done. Do not hesitate to request help when you require assistance.

Put your best foot forward. Inventively: Utilize your creativity to express yourself by paintings, writing or playing music. Utilizing art as a method to express sympathy could provide a sense of calm and comfort.

Moving forward

The process of healing from grief is an ongoing process which does not have a specific timeframe. But, in the end it is possible to do the following in order to progress:

Finding Meaning A common results of grieving is reflection. There is a chance that you have to reconsider your goals as well as your principles and your driving force in the world. The opportunity may be there to reflect and revive your internal compasses.

Setting achievable goals: When you're grieving for your loss, make sure you establish achievable objectives. It's possible to regain control of your life and return to your regular routine by devising an approach that is kid-friendly to get your life and routine to be back on track.

The ability to help: Talking to a professional or mentor can be beneficial when you are in a situation which cause a lot of discomfort or discomfort that happens near home. They could provide specific survival tips that will help you get over your luck.

Accepting trust: During the final moments of mourning the trust issue will come up regardless of whether it may be difficult initially. Since it allows you to determine when the burden of the tragedy will become easier to handle, trust can be the most effective way to strengthen.

Accepting that you are unhappy after a setback an emotional and deeply personal moment. Knowing the phases of grieving, implementing methods of survival and seeking aid will enable you to sort out the chaotic scene of grieving and help you think through the best way to repair, rebuild or move on. Although it is difficult but in the end it could lead to profound self-awareness and change.

The Resignation and Sadness as part of a relation

Rinstead of being just an unresolved feeling of pain the sadness may be an arduous path to giving up.

It can be hard to part with your connections with individuals or circumstances that matter for you after they have passed out of your life. Another thing to think about is the way in which lamenting can be understood as a method of surrender

Recognizing the reality of misfortune Acknowledging the real-world impact of misfortune is the first step towards being able to express regret. Similar to recognizing that the friendship you once were a part of is no longer aspect of your daily life. This can be a challenging but crucial phase in surrendering.

Reliving the Past A well-known part of grieving is reminiscing about your past interactions with someone or someone you lost and reliving your the past.

This is an opportunity for you to make the past come to the end of its journey and let it the past go, regardless of whether it's an unnecessary burden. You're letting it go. even if the memories you cherish will last and remain with you, the connection to the future you share in them has been lost.

The establishment of the close-to-home Connection The process of weeping is deeply personal process. In the course of grieving there is a variety of emotions, and then release these. The restorative, profound release will help free yourself from the bonds of home that bind yourself to items that you've lost.

Speaking About What was The act of lamenting isn't an equivalent of abandoning the cause; it is about reflecting to the past.

It can be done through rituals, memorial services or just simply appreciating the importance of things that you've lost as well as the positive features of your relationship.

Understanding the importance of change and its significance The most significant change is often triggered by suffering. Sometimes, it forces to reconsider your beliefs and your purpose for life. As you go through this it is possible to get rid of your old goals and embrace the new ones that will aid your growth and healing.

Conclusion and Acknowledgment

In the end, acknowledgement and the feeling of relief signal the conclusion of the grieving process. This is a feeling of knowing that although pain will not completely disappear but managing it becomes more manageable. The acknowledgment of this is a blessing which gives you confidence to keep going.

The process of grieving is a phase in development

There is a possibility of viewing mourning as a stalemate and a memorable time. It doesn't matter if it's painful or not, there's the possibility of improvement

Home near you Strength It is possible to become stronger and more resilient when you lose a close friend and family member. It is possible to handle uncomfortable and arousing feelings, which increases the resistance you have to setbacks in life.

The expanded empathy of mourning could aid you in becoming an empathetic and compassionate person towards your fellow mourners and individuals. The process can lead to relationships that are more empathetic and understanding.

New Life Needs: If you release yourself from things that aren't satisfying the way you feel, you might see a shift in your requirements. It is a first step towards being more satisfied and become more aware of what is important.

There is no reason to expect to begrudge or minimize the significance of who or what you've lost. The issue lies in acknowledging the loss, offering an apology for your loss as well as reviving your spirits and making progress through the healing process. It is possible that pain will eventually trigger forward progress and growth for humanity.

Find the healing and faith

After the initial and difficult stages of grieving, it is at this point that the process of healing and trusting is not just possible, but vital.

Even though moping is often an extremely unpleasant experience but it can also be an opportunity for growth improvement, and healing. In the aftermath of a disaster, you are able to find these methods to find healing and confidence:

Affirming Desire to Rise When you are in the middle of agony, it can appear impossible to imagine when the pain ceases. But, in the end, trust will find ways to bounce back. In the beginning, it could begin by displaying no signs of hope and a feeling that your lasting is diminishing, or a desire to live your living. You can allow yourself to be aware the signs of prosperity and celebrate this signal.

Setting reasonable Goals When you begin your journey with your plan, be sure to set realistic goals to you. Through these arguments, you will be able to gain control and regain your sense of reason.

It doesn't need to be difficult They can be just as simple as establishing an everyday schedule and self-care routines and implementing with the most well-known method of beginning over.

Engage in positive movements by participating in activities that raise your spirits and makes you feel great. This may involve regaining previously-loved hobbies, discovering new ones, or simply enjoying the sun's rays. Participating in activities that are beneficial can increase your satisfaction and help you recover.

Helpful and Effective: Weeping may cause a lot of problems in some circumstances and can cause extreme suffering in the home. Talking to a professional or a teacher could be helpful.

They can offer specific methods to help with reducing anxiety as you explore more complex or complex topics, as well as creating strategies to cope with stressful scenarios.

Accepting Development: Adversity may cause a dramatic growth in self-awareness. When you look at your own expectations and life You will find an increased sense of what you are doing and a more fervent determination to lead a wholesome existence. It can trigger improvement and growth in your self.

Connect with your Steady Connections: In the course of recovery, be reliant on your current network of people who are emotionally supportive in addition to any new ones you'll be able to create.

A calming presence as well as an understanding ear from your the family, friends, or support groups is a possibility. Friendships that provide support could be a source of assistance as you get towards recovering.

In relation to the memory: Honouring your memories of those items or people that you've lost is the same as giving up. Create rituals or gifts to acknowledge the positive elements of your friendship and the importance of your left. It could be a crucial part of healing.

Acceptance and Conclusion: After having overcome the depressive phases and reminiscing about your luck and experience the feeling of that everything is at an ending. The truth is that while the pain of luck may never be gone, managing it becomes more manageable. The acknowledgment of this is a blessing which gives you confidence to continue.

Self-empathy is a must. Depression isn't an indicator of weakness. there is no clear pattern. This shows the strength of your bond and love.

Develop self-sympathy as well as acceptance as you confront your way through the difficult process in healing and grief.

Making amends and rebuilding trust in the aftermath of a setback takes patience, self-care and patience. The process has the possibility to end up with an everyday life filled with opportunities and a positive outlook of the future with a new sense of the importance of life and personal development.

Chapter 7: Breaking Dangerous Links

Recognizing the Intoxicating Connections

Identifying the negative connection is probably the initial step towards the most well-known method of getting rid of.

It is essential to differentiate harmful relationships from ones that are healthy as they can affect the mental and spiritual health of your loved ones. When you are in a toxic relationship There are several distinct signs that you should be cognizant of

Continuously negative energy If you're involved in a toxic relationship you are likely to feel depleted and tense, or depressed. If you feel constantly unhappy when you're with someone it could be a sign of a negative relationship.

Respect for one another is necessary to maintain a healthy relationship. If someone repeatedly disregards your values, boundaries, or norms, then that's an alarming sign.

Manipulative Behaviors: Lying manipulating or lying strategies are just a few tactics used by poisonous people to maintain you or your situation in check. They might even participate in games in order in order to keep the control.

Conflicts that are not resolved: In unhealthy relationships, disagreements can be in confusion or even cause further the problem. A successful correspondence or compromise is often not enough.

Inequitable Giving: If you often lend a helping assistance, offer support or do rituals of piety for them and do not expect anything back Your relationship might be unhealthful and insecure.

Conclusive Analysis: People who are poisonous are likely to constantly challenge, limit or denigrate your. The words or actions they use could lead to your confidence diminish.

Distinction: Spending time with harmful people could make you feel dependent as well as separating them from family and friends. It is possible to identify harmful relationships by using this technique.

Types of A savage behavior, regardless of whether physical, verbal or even psychological, can be the sign of a toxic relationship. The most obvious example is of requesting help and support.

Insanity: Bad relationships can hinder an individual's ability to improve and develop. Be aware of your relationship based on the idea you feel pressured or do not have the ability to achieve the goals you have set and desire.

Unsafe Help: People can offer assistance at times that are appropriate for them. But they might not offer it in the time you're most desperate for the assistance. The situation could turn out to end up being incredibly unpleasant.

The recognition of warning signals is the first stage in recognizing that an unhealthy relationship could be a problem. It's essential to go with the advice of your intuition and focus on your happiness. After recognizing that you're in a negative relation is to determine the best way to deal with it and, if it is necessary stop it to protect your mental well-being and wellbeing.

Method for setting Boundaries and cutting off a plethora of bad connections

The decision to end toxic relationships can be difficult, however taking the steps necessary to ensure your progress and success is equally crucial. Here are a few strategies for setting limits and ending bad relationships:

Self-Reflection: Review your relationship with the other person and what it means on your life. Think about your most important wants as well as your values and overall wellbeing. Being aware is crucial for the direction you take.

Make Your Boundaries Clear If you believe it's likely that your connection will be successful, you should consider making clear and firm limits. After you've shared your expectations and your assumptions, prepare to implement them.

Reduce Contact: Avoid to talk with the harmful person for too long. In this way you will be able to promote clarity and separation from the home near to home.

You should think about ignoring or stopping following the rules and guidelines regarding online entertainment and communication.

Ask for Help: Contact your family members, friends, or a therapist for continuous assistance and advice. Speak to trustworthy friends regarding your worries and feelings will help you feel reassured and help you gain an objective view.

Establish an Robust Organization Create a strong organization: Form the people in your life that will be there for you should your relationship break down. You will be less enthused of being required to work at home or be with the person who is toxic.

Self-care and exercise: Make taking care of yourself your main priority if wish to ensure the health of your body and mind. Relax, relieve stress or calming activities.

Alerts to Perceive: Always be attentive to behavior and interactions that attract the attention of harm. Be alert to such warning indicators can help when making sound decisions when it comes to establishing a connection.

Make sure you have documentation in the rare event that you're insecure about your security or require legal assurance you may find it beneficial in certain situations to record any negative conduct.

Plan Your Time Off: When you are deciding to part ways with your pal, make use of clever takeoff maneuvering. This strategy can include realistic actions like moving to a new home or updating your contact info.

It is important to clearly define what the consequences will be These are the consequences if the person who is dangerous continues to push the limits be sure that the actions are a consequence. You must be prepared to accept the consequences of their actions.

"No contact rule": the most effective option in some instances is to be completely quiet. It means cutting any communication and ties with the victim. While it is challenging, it is often essential for your progress.

Legal Activities When you are in a danger situation and you need to take the legal route, you might be required to consider obtaining the restraining order, or even contacting police.

Find Effective Help When the relationship appears to be particularly harmful or toxic You should seek assistance from an expert or mentor. They may offer strategies to deal with difficult circumstances and coping with the emotional consequences of breaking up with a toxic partner.

It is important to remember that ending a harmful relationship is a self-defense and self-care step. However, it could also be a test. This is crucial for your success as well as personal growth. Every day life needs to be filled with fulfilling as well as empowering connections.

Rebuilding after letting go

A Though letting go emotional attachments, relationships that are toxic and other negative elements of your life might be difficult, it could open up the possibility of the best future.

Beginning over and recalibration is a major part of this process. You can re-build and lead more joyful, happier living by doing these things:

Helpful and self-sufficient

Make a list of your personal needs. Examine your physical and spiritual assets. Give yourself permission to grieve and heal, since it's essential to do for the sake of moving over the old.

Connect with your own inner self in order in order to restore your character. Think about your argument, beliefs and aspirations. Make use of this chance to review your objectives and the characteristics you have.

Establish a Help Organization

Use the networks of family and friends and others who will offer emotional support. Let them be a part of your recovery.

Share your thoughts and emotions with trusted people. Be a good and trustworthy person: Place your personal needs prior to your own needs. Take a look at your wealth as spiritual and monetary. It is important to be grieving and healing since this is vital for moving on from your previous.

For a return to your persona connect to your self-image. Consider your reasons of your values, beliefs, and personal preferences. Make the most of this opportunity to review your character and goals.

Establish a Help Organization

Use the networks of your family and friends as well as other people who are able to help you through your emotional struggles. Allow them to aid with your recovery. Share your thoughts and emotions with trusted people.

Make New goals

Assess your ambitions and goals. Review the goals you've established for yourself. When you create new, important objectives, you may gain motivation and conviction.

Create a routine

Create a plan for your day which encourages consistency and stability. The consistency of a routine could allow you to feel at ease and relaxed while healing.

Examine New Interests

Find new hobbies or hobbies that grab your interest. It could result in more interests or connections to like-minded friends.

Expert Support

It's worth getting help from a professional if you're struggling to cope emotionally triggered issues that come from the decision to let go. Counselling or therapy is a highly effective tool to heal as well as self-improvement.

I apologize. When one practices forgiveness, it is possible to let go of the past as well as self. The word "forgiveness" does not mean you accept the behavior of people who are toxic however it does free the emotional burdens and allows you to continue your life.

Set Limits

When you are healing, establish limits that are reasonable in your relationships. Be sure to maintain the self-esteem you have and ensure your psychological well-being.

Accept Change

Maintain an open-minded attitude to the latest developments and situations. While change may be difficult, it can also provide the possibility of improvement and change in a person's life.

Discover Meaning

Get the most meaning from your experience. Sometimes, adversity can teach you important lessons that can help you for the next time.

Salute Little Victories

Celebrate the tiny victories as well as the progress you've accomplished so to this point. Even if they are small the accomplishment, acknowledging and recognizing your achievements can help boost the motivation of you and increase your feeling of self-worth.

Be Mindful

Find mindfulness to stay fully active in your life. Mindfulness allows you to enjoy life's small moments and relish its most memorable occasions.

Find Inspiration

Find inspiration from your guides, books, or anyone else who has been through hardship and have made an impressive life change. Your path may be inspired and guided from their stories.

Remember that building after having let go is entirely yours. Although there may be challenges and setbacks throughout the journey, the situation could improve and the next chapter could be more positive.

Be calm, remain determined to improve your health and provide an open welcome to this new chapter of your life.

Parting with material Goods

The Relationship Between Material Possessions and Attachment

Your self-esteem as well as your overall wellbeing are frequently dependent on our possessions. Becoming aware of the relationship between material possessions and attachment is essential to master the art of let go.

This is where we examine the relationship between us and how it impacts our lives:

It's the Identity Trap: Our possessions can shape our identity. They're often the way that we convey to people around us our position as morally upright, a person of character, and so on. It can be difficult to let go of possessions, without being able to give up a little of our self.

Emotional attachments: We typically assign our possessions an emotional meaning. These items could be a symbol of the owner's affection and care, hold emotional value or are associated with memories of a lifetime. Removal of these items could trigger strong emotions.

The Consumer Culture: In today's society that is driven by the consumer, having goods is extremely valued. Peer pressure and advertising reinforce the notion that possessions are essential to happiness and prosperity. It could result in an uneasy attachment to physical possessions.

The stress and clutter of space get more crowded as people accumulate numerous items. This can lead to overstress and stress. The stress could indicate that your relationship with objects is causing harm to the health of your.

Environmental Impact The main reasons for environmental problems is the overuse of items that are not essential. Recognizing this can encourage people to stop using things that aren't significant or necessary.

Achieving Fulfillment The common belief is that buying a lot of stuff brings happiness and satisfaction. But, the reality of this pursuit often exposes how unreliable these bonds have become, leaving individuals in a state of desperation and despair.

The Minimalist Movement: This movement is about getting rid of useless items in order to lead in a more simple life.

It focuses on the fact that happiness and fulfillment result from genuine interactions and experiences instead of possessions.

Finance Freedom: Becoming excessively materialism can lead to stress in the financial realm. Reduce your credit and save cash by donating items that you don't need anymore.

To declutter and simplify your lifestyle, be aware of the relationship between possessions of material and emotional. It is possible to begin letting things that no longer serve to you, and live the simpler, happier lifestyle by understanding the cultural, psychological as well as emotional elements that make up this connection.

Methodologies to eliminate trash and streamlining

Departing from material possessions may aid in simplifying and reorganizing your lifestyle, which could bring about transformations as well as liberating moments. Here are a few tips for effective decluttering and simplifying

Set out your objectives Set your objectives in decluttering. What are the goals you're thinking of? You may want to reduce the clutter in your lifestyle, reduce the stress levels or even improve the design of your house having a clear set of goals will assist you in achieving them.

Begin with a small project: Renovating the whole living area in one go can be overwhelming. Start with a smaller area that you can use as an example, such as a drawer or maybe a small space. If you can see the benefits of organizing, you'll be more driven to carry on.

The Twelve-Month Rule stipulates that an item is deemed to be clearance-worthy in the event that it isn't employed or used during the whole year. This guideline helps you evaluate the worth of your possessions.

Type-by-Type Sorting of Trash: Separate your items that you want to get rid of into groups (e.g. clothing and kitchenware, cookbooks and so on.). This Marie Kondo method helps to organize the process and manageable.

Donate or sell: Think about giving in good condition items to charities or selling them through online. The knowledge that your possessions will be used for something else could simplify the process of selling them.

Follow The KonMari method: Marie Kondo says that you should keep items that "spark happiness." The time is now to give up items when they does not bring you joy anymore or is a necessity for your daily life.

The Four-Box Method You can divide your items into four sections: "Donate," "Keep," "Trash," and "Undecided." It is easier to make decisions with this technique.

Digital Declutter: Sort through everything you have on your computer including the files on your computer, your email inboxes, as well as social network accounts. Clean up your digital file and unsubscribe from unneeded emails, and make sure you are able to manage your relationships with social networks.

Suggestions for Assistance: Ask help from a family member or a family member. Sometimes, the difficult job of deciding which items to keep and what to throw away can be facilitated through an objective viewpoint.

Establish boundaries: You should not keep too many items in a particular grouping. Choose, for instance, that you'll only have five books, or ten pair of sneakers. You are forced to make use of judgment.

Make sure you take care to give away your sensitive Things: Letting go of precious items is one of the most difficult tasks. Take note of their significance over time. If you'd like to save the sentimental value while preserving the object think about taking pictures of them and putting together an album of memories.

Create new purchasing routines after decluttering, you can spend more thoughtfully. Beware of impulse buying and limit your spending to things that actually improve your life.

Maintenance and regular check-ins Regular check-ins and maintenance of your belongings frequently will assist you in avoiding the clutter. Check-ins regularly to clear clutter helps to prevent accumulation of useless objects.

Focus on the Positives: All through the process, keep in mind about the benefits of reducing and decluttering. These include a easier to manage and a more peaceful household, financial savings as well as the ability to concentrate on what is really matter.

Honor Your Achievements Honor Your Achievements: Celebrate your accomplishments as well as the actions you make to reduce the burden of your daily life. The willingness to make any sacrifices is the first step toward living a more relaxed and more fulfilling life.

De-cluttering and simplifying doesn't only involve giving away tangible items but also altering one's perspective to lead an easier and more fulfilling living.

If you implement these ideas in practice, you can alter your space and outlook, allowing space for things that really are important.

Be Joyful in the Embrace of Simplicity

The practice of minimalism may result in an immense sense of satisfaction and happiness. Below are a few reasons the simple lifestyle you live can be a great way to feel happier.

A less cluttered home, more space Clearing out your space is an essential part of minimalism. It will make the home appear calm and open. If the space is free of clutter and you feel it, you will experience the peace and tranquility that it brings.

Take time for what really Matters: Minimalism encourages you to be focused on items, people, and relationships that truly make you happy. The shift in perspective will allow you to spend greater time and attention on most important things.

Financial Independence: By cutting down on expenditures that are unnecessary and removing the requirement for huge storage areas, minimalism may assist in becoming financially stable. Being free of the burden of financial debt can be more peaceful and happier.

When it comes to minimalism, purchases are advised to be conducted in a way that is mindful. Each purchase is an intentional purchase that can lead to larger and more important purchases. The idea is that you should prioritize quality over quantity.

Ample Time to Experience More Time for Experiences: You'll have more time to travel activities, fun, moments of joy as well as other pursuits that will enhance your lifestyle and increase your growth by spending less time organising and maintaining your belongings.

Reduction of the impact on our planet A minimalist life style is eco-friendly and less harmful to the planet. Feel happier and happier by reducing your impact on the environment.

More Relationships: Living an easy lifestyle can lead to stronger, more intimate bonds with people. The feeling of fulfillment and fulfillment will grow when you put more effort and effort into the relationships you have with others.

You can pursue your passions with freedom The minimalist lifestyle frees you of the weight of items, which allows you to spend more time and energy on your interests and interests.

A simplified daily Routine A simple routine makes the little things in life simpler. Being able to keep less clutter can make your routine less rushed and organized.

The importance of gratitude for the present Living a life that is simple can help you develop gratitude for what is happening now. It is possible to learn to appreciate your present moment and appreciate the beauty of the smallest things.

Relaxation: Giving go of the desire to acquire more possessions may result in a deep feeling of peace and contentment. It is a fact that you have everything you require.

Reduced Decision Fatigue: because you are less cluttered and less stuff to carry around, you're less stressed out when making choices. It is not necessary to lose precious time or effort on trivial decisions. Instead, you can focus on what is most important.

Chapter 8: The Giving Up Of Any Presence To Limit Thoughts

Accepting and spreading beliefs that Challenge Oneself

Self-restricting mental beliefs are those which hinder us from achieving our potential to the maximum and leading fulfilling life.

It is important to recognize these thoughts, and then face them to allow the thought go. It's that simple.

Self-Reflection: Before you begin think about your goals along with your goals and the areas where you are stuck. Examine the thoughts and emotions that are which are hindering you from making progress. For a change to occur the way you think, first one has to learn to become aware.

Use Differential Examples: Be cautious when you are reciting your thoughts about instances. What is the negative thought which keep appearing to you? Are they affecting confidence in yourself and stopping your from making a decision?

Find out if different influences, like social, family or any other involvement have influenced the beliefs. Be aware that it's impossible for you to keep the beliefs you have.

Doubting the validity of these assertions make them seem vague. They could claim they're supported by unquestionable evidence, or can be said to mean that they're merely preposterous assumptions or even tensions? Examine whether, overall it is commonplace and well-established.

Get Advice: Talk to your mentors, friends, or professionals to obtain an alternate view. You might be able to discern in the thoughts of others self-limiting beliefs which you weren't aware of.

Switch out to enthralling Convictions When you've figured out what beliefs you hold restrict you in your own mind, attempt to change them into ones which will provide you with more credibility.

For example, you could substitute the sentence "I'm insufficient" by "I'm always learning and improving."

Utilize fascinating certifications to keep your newly-formed self-empowering belief system. Repetition these affirmations regularly to assist you in restructuring your thinking patterns.

Image Achievement: Imagine yourself achieving your goals, and being motivated to make progress. With the help of a visual representation this can boost your confidence, and decrease your doubts about yourself.

Care and thinking: Engage in activities that help you to improve your understanding of the world around you. Through meditation, you will be able to build a mental space to changing and get rid of instances of unlogical reasoning.

Set small goals Make small, achievable targets to challenge your own beliefs about yourself. Once you have achieved the goals you set, confidence in yourself increases.

Find bright models. Look for people who have succeeded in the face of opposing views. The inspiration and the motivation that comes from the interactions of these people could prove beneficial.

Be aware of the possibility for failure as an opportunity gain knowledge and improve. Accept that mistakes constitute a vital part in learning. Take failures as a chance to grow rather than an affirmation of your limitations.

Responsibility is a complex issue: Talk about your goals with a trusted companion or friend that can assist you in overcoming your self-limiting thoughts and view yourself as a person who is accountable.

Be Respectful of Your Achievements Respect Your Achievements: Be proud of your achievements, regardless of how they are.

Your achievements provide a wake-up alarm for your new, affirming ideas.

Helpful Assistance Effective Assistance: If you are suffering from unhelpful or deeply embedded self-limiting belief systems, it is advisable consult an expert or counsellor. They will be able to provide you with specific strategies to disprove and challenge the assumptions.

Refusing to accept and challenge self-limiting thoughts could be a game changer. To replace old concepts with new and empowering concepts that increase the self-confidence and achievement of yours You must remain compassionate and gentle with yourself.

Methods to modify thought processes

Enhancing the capacity to modify thoughts patterns, especially those that are self-limiting, is vital for personal and professional growth. With these techniques it is possible to alter your mental images:

Careful deeds You will see your thoughts with a clearer perspective as you think about them. Through showing compassion, will be able to recognize your thinking and take decisions that will help you refocus on a positive path.

CBT is one of the forms of psychotherapy for the mind. It helps patients identify and defeat negative concepts through the aid of a particular kind of therapy. The help of a specialist will allow you to review and change your notions with better ones.

Make and tell stories which challenge your self-limiting beliefs to eliminate negative ones. In order to seem more assured and confident such as, say, changing it into "I'm confident and skilled."

Journaling: Record your thoughts and feelings into your notebook. It will help you pinpoint what's behind your scattered ideas. After identifying the root cause it is possible to make modifications.

The ABCDE Method A cognitive-behavioral therapy method breaks down beliefs into enactment of events results, convictions questions, as well as novel impacts.

The practice is often used. Change your mental beliefs by examining your assumptions and the implications they bring.

Representation: Place yourself in a circumstance of seriously altering and redefining your thought patterns. If you're free from the thoughts that limit you, imagine your positive impact on your life to come.

Join a circle with Positive People: Gather an organization of colleagues who influence your outlook. Their confidence is likely to profoundly influence how you view the world.

Get educated about the mental tendencies that influence your thoughts, including the tendency to catastrophize and preferring safe information. By gaining a better understanding of these tendencies, you will be able to identify and overcome these.

Set clear goals by defining specific achievable goals, you'll be able to concentrate on making significant progress towards improving your self-awareness, and not worrying about the wrong thinking routines.

The ability to feel empathy for yourself: be very forgiving to yourself to show compassion for yourself. Be kind to yourself while trying to change the habits you have cultivated. Be aware that this is a method.

Study Personal Improvement Handbooks Read self-help guides and other resources for improving your self by inspiring courage, as well as altering the way one thinks. They typically provide enlightening techniques and workouts.

Attractive: Spellbinding is helpful for people who are changing their thinking patterns. An experienced hypnotic expert will guide you through the process of changing your psyche and mind.

Reputation and input: Discuss your goals with a mentor or a close friend who you count on for helpful feedback. Also, be aware that you're accountable to change your thinking.

Be open to your inner dialogue and stop focusing on negative self-talk. Be aware of your inner dialogue and fight self-talk that is critical.

Refuse to think about any negative thoughts that you have in your mind with something fascinating and amazing at the time.

Recognize Progress: Regardless of the small improvements have been, recognize and praise your achievements. A positive critique can motivate you to take your plan further.

Find out how changing your mental experiences is a constant pattern that requires patience and perseverance. Empathize with your self and stay determined to follow your own path of actions and support from the government.

If you are persistently practicing and employ the appropriate strategies, it's feasible to transform one's thinking habits to lead a more pleasant and fulfilling life.

Promoting an Optimal Developmental View

Promoting progress is a powerful technique for dispersing and changing restricting thoughts is through the perspective. Development outlook refers to an idea that, if you are accountable and put in the effort to improve your capabilities and knowledge. How to revive an outlook that is geared towards development:

Accept Requirements: Look at the obstacles as opportunities to become more efficient. See your obstacles as opportunities to develop at the time whenever they occur.

Think of your work as the Way to Power: Be aware that your ability to learn is heavily dependent on the work you do. What you perform increases your capacity to achieve some thing.

Learn from setbacks: Consider setbacks as an important instance rather than as a criticism of your capabilities. Examine what went wrong, and apply the understanding you've acquired to analyse and fix it.

Believe in the Power of Yet If you have to cross the line of a wall, be sure to add "yet" when you make your argument. Instead of thinking "I cannot do this" such as, for instance consider thinking "I am not able to do this now." The slight change in phonetics suggests that you're still learning.

Look for opportunities with the capacity to instruct your something new. Keep an in mind opportunities to develop as an individual. Take part in courses, classes or even independent studies for a broadening of your perspectives and skills.

Focus your attention on the interactions instead of the end result in honoring the process. Enjoy the self-awareness and education method. When you are working through your work, the end result will be clear.

Find Out More Details: Recognize the constructive criticism as a chance to develop. Get feedback from your the coach, your supervisor, or others to enhance your understanding and skills.

Beware of negative self-talk When you are being doubtful about your abilities or thinking in a critical manner take these negative thoughts with a straight face. Make them well-planned and growth-oriented beliefs.

Be Observant: Recognize and celebrate every one of your small however significant wins during the course of. Recognizing your achievements can help keep your growth mindset.

Create a positive mental attitude through observation and understanding of those who demonstrate this. Study their stories, struggles as well as their successes in order to improve your own journey.

Learn from Others: Sharing your expertise with other people will aid in understanding the current situation, and help you build your mental capacity to develop. Engage with people in discussions about your thoughts and experiences.

Be open to new ideas: Be open to new ideas and ideas. Make the most of your opportunity to gain from a variety of sources and contacts immediately.

Stay interested: Maintain curiosity. Engage in questions and give efforts to gain a greater comprehension. Inspiring curiosity drives enthusiasm for learning.

Move forward. Recognize the importance of effort and perseverance essential to advancement. Do not give up in confronting of difficulties or adversity. The ability to persevere is the most important aspect of an attitude to develop.

You can see your goals being achieved Perceptual exercises can assist you in achieving the goals you set. Through visualization, your excitement and confidence can increase.

The development of a growth mindset can be an empowering relationship that allows people to transcend their limitations and explore possibilities to grow professionally and personally. The result could be an increased sense of self-confidence as well as a sense of adaptability and confidence.

Chapter 9: Accepting The Risk As Well As The Adaptability

The inevitable change in life

The most essential element of living in the present moment and life experience of humans is the constant change. Accepting and understanding change's character is the very first step in embracing change. Because of this, changes are an integral part of living.

Normal movement: Every day, life shows signs of evolution. There are various levels of growth, development and metamorphosis, starting right from birth to the point of death. The process of change is an essential part of the process.

Natural Movements: Everything that is in the world around us changes constantly. Weather changes, seasons change, weather changes, and so does the climate. The need for transition is to move through these interruptions.

Self-improvement: Improvement can be directly linked to awareness of oneself and disclosure. Experiments, that are inherently changing, allow people to grow as they learn and change.

Social and social changes Social and social order are also subject to long-term changes. The entire world as well as our own people particularly are constantly developing due to innovative concepts, breakthroughs in technology as well as artistic inventions.

New and innovative advancements in the field of money: The economy and innovation are growing rapidly together. Because of advances and developments, individuals and professional circles will face different challenges and new possibilities.

Relations, whether close, intimate or extremely emotional develop naturally and change as time passes. More vibrant and stronger relationships can be created by adjusting to the changes in our world.

Health and longevity The body undergoes significant changes when we grow older. Being able to adapt and being aware of the risks are crucial to keeping your health.

Employment and Career in the age of professionals, no thing stays identical. Individuals must be able to adapt and develop different skills as business, industries, or the roles they play in change.

The deep and thoughtful motions: Mental and emotional states are constantly changing and fluid. It's crucial to be aware of and regulate these behaviors so that you can recognize people as they actually are.

Events that are global in nature like pandemics and financial declines, or apocalyptic events can result in drastic and unanticipated changes. The ability to adjust to the changing circumstances is the most important aspect of flexibility.

Recognizing the fact that change is inevitable provides individuals the capacity to be stronger, more resilient and adaptable. A positive outlook places adaptability to change over the fear of or resistance. The acceptance of change as a vital element of life will lead to self-actualization, a greater perception of control, as well as optimism about the future.

How to handle empathy and vulnerability

Although it can be challenging, managing the emotions of anxiety and sensitivity is a crucial skill to master for being able to accept changes. Below are some strategies to manage these thoughts:

Awareness and concern: Remain at the moment and observe the feelings you feel of fear and vulnerability as you engage in exercises for caring. Accept that these feelings are normal and part of the human experience.

Make a list of your fears Consider your particular anxieties and fears that you feel. First, you must identify the things you're afraid of so that you can overcome your fears.

Stay updated: If you are you are in doubt, search to reliable sources for information, and keep your cool. The knowledge gained can ease your anxiety and give you the feeling of being in control.

Be able to make sense of your assumptions Take note of many weaknesses that cannot be fixed. Instead of try to reduce uncertainty and be focused on fully understanding your reaction to it.

Pay attention to the factors that can be influenced by you Decide which issues you can influence for your ward and then take the appropriate actions. You may feel a stronger result from this.

Maintain Flexibility Promote diversity and flexibility. Unexpected turns occur as often as they are possible to encounter in everyday life while vulnerability can be simpler to discover in a person who is flexible.

Positive Self-Talk and Gratitude Eliminate your negative self-talk, and replace it with affirming and positive thoughts. Believe in yourself and believe that you're adept at overcoming challenges and conquering your vulnerability.

Get help: ask to be assisted by an expert, a friend or a your family member. Chatting with somebody about your concerns and worries can allow you to gain perspective and feel more secure.

Self-care that is safe: Choose practices that help reduce stress and promote overall well-being the top priority. Introspection, exercise, distractions and time spent with family and friends are just some examples.

Limit your exposure to stressors Avoid situations that cause you to become more anxious or uneasy in times of greater erraticness. It could mean the need to put off online information or entertainment for a time.

Make the Present a priority Instead of thinking about apocalyptic future events focus on the present situation. Be careful and keep an "presently" focus can reduce the anxiety and fear.

Recognize your learning Make the most of uncertainty as an opportunity to grow. The tragedy is not just useful as a teacher and a great motivator, but it is also able to encourage self-awareness.

Image: Positive outcomes In spite of your vulnerability make use of representational exercises to aid you in imagining reactions and outcomes that are successful. It can help you look at the future from an positive perspective.

Try to build Strength The ability to face challenges. This skill can allow you to improve your ability to handle uncertainty.

Seek out skilled assistance Seek assistance from a professional in mental health in the event that you think your financial well-being is adversely affected by stress and apprehension. They will be able to provide assistance and techniques for stress reduction that are that are specific to your needs.

Being able to cope with the vulnerability and fear will assist to eventually adapt despite it being something that is deeply embedded in your brain. It is possible to maintain an energised, secure and confident presence through accepting that change is an integral part of your life and developing strategies to cope with the uncertainty and fear that it can bring.

Sturdiness and flexibility

You must be able to adapt and flexible to explore vulnerability and changes efficiently. This article will help you foster and develop these traits:

Build your ability for critical thinking: To approach the issues with a focus on solutions and develop your thinking abilities. Break down problems into steps, and look at different strategies.

Think of a challenge as a chance to improve in your self-awareness. Recall the challenges you've had to face in the past as well as your successes in overcoming them.

Utilize the information you've acquired about enhancing flexibility. Encourage a development mindset Take a growth-oriented approach which sees obstacles as opportunities to learn and grow. Believe in your abilities to learn and change.

Keep a strong emotional connection Establish a Supportive Emotional Network in times of uncertainty you can rely on family members and network of emotional friends. The sharing of your emotions and thoughts to others can be soothing as well as motivating.

Maintain a positive outlook by focusing on your strengths as well as your previous achievements. Positive outlook can assist you to become more adaptable and conquer the obstacles.

Keep yourself flexible and agile by being open to new concepts and approaches. Stay flexible and adaptable to changes in the environment and changing your strategies as required.

Self-compassion: Be kind and patient towards yourself. Accept that it may be challenging to make the necessary adjustments to change and vulnerability, and going through uncertain times is not unusual.

Set achievable, functional goals If you are facing changes, set achievable, functional objectives. When more significant goals are reduced into smaller, more manageable goals, they might seem more manageable.

Accept your disappointment. Instead of viewing the experience as something to avoid, consider using the experience as an opportunity for growth. Enhance your method using the knowledge learned from your mistakes.

Enhance your ability to perceive the people you meet by recognizing and managing your feelings. This allows you to appreciate people with greater depth. This is essential to effectively manage change and apprehension.

Find occasions to utilize your capabilities to be adaptable. This might mean engaging in new work or altering your everyday routine to deal with unexpected situations.

Be informed: Staying up-to-date in uncertain times will give an impression of control, and help you navigate the fluctuating cycle.

Don't get caught up in overanalyzing. Steer away from a lot of thinking and thinking. Instead, focus in taking action and moving forward, even if just small increments at an time.

Take advantage of change as an opportunity to grow: Despite the fact that changes can seem difficult initially consider it the chance to develop yourself. Through change, new perspectives and new experiences could emerge.

Get expert advice If you're experiencing difficulty improving your flexibility and adaptability at your own pace consider consulting with an expert or trainer. The strategies and guidance they provide are able to be adjusted to suit the specific needs of your.

The ability to adapt and be strong are qualities that are able to be developed and enhanced over the years. They aid you in accepting changes with confidence and navigate uncertain situations with confidence.

It is possible to continue living a an enduring, fluid, and fulfilling existence by actively embracing these traits.

Chapter 10: A Life That Is Purpose-Driven

Identifying your Personality and Interests

Recognizing your strengths and interests can be a significant step toward being a more intentional person. Utilize these strategies to begin the process of self-disclosing:

Self-Reflection: Consider your reasons for being satisfied and happy in the reflection of your personal experiences and actions. Choose the aspects that will influence your life.

Explore new Pursuits Explore and test something new, perhaps even one that you might not have thought of or considered in the past. Test and error could be employed to uncover undiscovered areas of interest.

Previous Interests: Think back to your past interests or activities that you were able to enjoy. In some cases, they may provide the opportunity to pursue your passions.

Assessment of Values Set your own mind on your primary convictions. Which values and ideals that are essential to you? In the majority of cases the choices you make and your goals depend on your values.

Be aware of your inner Voice: Identify your own inner voice and the direction you are following. Sometimes, your intuition might reveal the real passions of your heart are.

Look for inspiration from others that inspire you, or who have extraordinary experiences. It may be beneficial to understand your personal activities and goals by observing instances from their experience.

Create the goals Make sure you set measurable goals that are compatible to your strengths and the areas you are interested in. The act of writing goals will help you get closer to living a life in line with the core purpose of your life.

Note: Write down a diary in which you record your thoughts, feelings or experiences as well as ideas. It could provide information about your beliefs and the your areas of fulfillment.

Talks: Discuss your hobbies and beliefs with your colleagues, your mentors or professionals who will help your journey through this phase. They may provide short explanations.

Inquiry and care Take time for care and contemplation to find peace within and clear. These strategies can help in the identification of your real requirements.

Give and volunteer in exchange serving others as well as helping the community may provide direction throughout your day. Consider participating with initiatives that will allow you to give back to your local community.

Consider the views from those who have been in contact with your personal situation. They may provide insight into your character or interests, as well as other characteristics that you're not in the loop.

Be a student and strive to learn Continue to study and research. Sometimes, education can result in the discovery of new ideas and dreams.

Illustration: Visualize you living the life of your desires, in which your personality and interests can be perfectly matched. It is helpful.

Reduce and get out: By getting rid of all distractions and clutter from your life, you'll be able to concentrate on what is important and uncover your true passions.

Finding your interests and beliefs could help you live an enjoyable, purposeful life. When you align your choices and actions with what is in tune with your values, everyday scheduling brings happiness and an underlying sense of joy.

What is the best way to get rid of stuff? can bring meaning to your Life

Allowing yourself to wander could lead to an empowering experience as well as a deeper presence.

The Time for Items to Arrive It is possible to release yourself from the burden that is pressing on you, by getting rid of old grievances, tensions and nagging fears. The insightful presentation is based on new experiences and possibilities that are in line with the goals you have set for yourself.

Clear Values: When you get rid of any relationships and other distractions that do not benefit your life, you are more conscious of your strengths and your priorities. Being clear is crucial for living a lifestyle that is aligned with your mission.

Being able to accept change: Sometimes losing hope means that you must learn to be vulnerable as well as change. Accepting change and keeping an open-minded mindset will allow to identify opportunities that are in alignment with the purpose of your life.

Self-awareness demands self-analysis and introspection. When you let off old ideas or plans and family relationships You become closer to your own self and the logic behind it.

Transferring Assets: By giving the things or pursuits which you'll never appreciate, you will be able to concentrate your efforts, time and funds to projects which are more in line to your personality and interests.

Lower Pressure: You could be feeling better and less stressed by letting go of things that won't be beneficial to you in the future. A peaceful, calm mind can identify and take on meaningful tasks.

Attitude to new Encounters Let off your relationships and expectations, you'll be more open to new experiences and opening doors. It is possible to decide what you want to accomplish in your life.

Continue to work at the present moment: Sometimes, letting go can mean breaking free of the bonds to the past or worries concerning the future. If you are able to fully remain in the present and the greater chance it is that you'll discover your goal.

The process of gaining legitimacy: Leaning into and accepting who you have to be requires you to give up. Being authentic is crucial to finding and achieving your purpose in life because it requires living your life according to your authentic self.

Influence on others: If you release the things you don't need You could be a source of inspiration for people around you. You have the ability to inspire others who are around you by your path in self-awareness and wisdom.

Prioritization and equilibrium: If you have to sacrifice something it is necessary to determine your priorities according to what's part of your everyday routine. This can result in an efficient and targeted utilization of the money you have invested.

Living with a Plan In getting rid of your things that distract you and responsibilities, you will be able to be more focused on your life. Each decision and every action has an objective, and this adds importance to your the way you live your life.

It is the qualities that help you resist losing hope, such as flexibility and adaptability, will aid you to overcome challenges and setbacks on your journey of living a life that is meaningful.

Discovering Your Passions and Resources: letting go could be an exploration which reveals your interests and what brings your the most pleasure.

Let go of the past to create space for the fresh is an act of surrender. It's about making the physical and mental space needed to let the passion of your heart be seen. If you are able to let go of things that won't be of any use to you You'll find that you're much more attune to who you truly are and what you are driven by to live your life.

Stories of real people who let go of their worries and realised that what they were looking for was crucial

Manyone who's realized their goals in life through abandoning. Some real-world examples can be found the following:

Marie Kondo

Marie Kondo, a Japanese designer and organizer, earned the attention of many due to her KonMari method for organizing and decluttering. Her philosophy is not focusing on material gain that doesn't offer "flash happiness."

In the course of her life she could aid others in cleaning their homes as well as helping others live more positive and fulfilling lives.

Oprah Winfrey

The tale of Oprah Winfrey provides an excellent instance of the time when one has to quit. Her life was a struggle that was marked in her early times by hardship and neediness and eventually became a moderator and media mogul, as well as the philanthropist.

In her efforts to use her foundation's power to inspire people to conquer barriers and lead their most fulfilling lives, Oprah's principal goal was evident.

When he was let go by the firm he founded, Steve Occupations, the famous and late leader of Mac experienced a profound emotion-driven shift in his situation. When he wasn't working and looking into other interests and decided to leave his commitment to Apple.

He finally made his return in Apple with a greater vision and new view. The result was that innovations such as Apple's iPhone and iPad have revolutionized the IT sector.

Nelson Mandela

The former South African president Nelson Mandela is an excellent instance of surrendering power favor of a truly remarkable amazing.

He fought to stop the government-sponsored racial segregation that was across South

Africa after being freed from prison for 27 years and telling the captors that the pardon was granted. He could have steered his country towards agreement and compromise, in letting go the anger and rage he felt.

Elizabeth Gilbert

Elizabeth Gilbert experienced a period of reflection and disconnection. Gilbert renounced the burden of her beliefs and obligations and began a new journey that was self-disclosure and discovery.

This experience prompted her bestseller book, as well as her teaching career as an essayist and lecturer.

Malala Yousafzai

An Pakistani educator and lobbyist, Malala gave up her fear of the Taliban as well as her connection to her typical childhood in order to promote girls in education. Although she was wounded in the head she fought on and continued to fight for that all children had access to education. She became the youngest person ever to receive the Nobel Prize.

Shetty Jay

A powerful speaker, former pastor Jay Shetty gave up a decent corporate job to live an exemplary life. His time as a priest has helped to discover the purpose of his life that is to share wisdom and help others live more fulfilled lives.

In order to discover what they are looking for on earth, people have to let go of all sorts of attachments, including things of the material world, beliefs about cultural values as well as painful memories of the past. They encourage others to contemplate what they could let go of to find their passion and make a significant impact on the world with their adventures.

Chapter 11: Anxiety Stress, Negative Idea

A person who is anxious is prone to frenzied, pessimistic and excessive stress-related sensations. Some people also experience real negative effects from tension such as the chest pain and shaking.

There's no one reason which triggers anxiety, fear, concept, or tension. Experts suggest that the feelings start with the mix of diverse variables. This includes genes and the external environment.

The thing that is evident as at present is that certain emotions, experiences and situations can trigger or attempt to eliminate nervousness's negative effects. The elements mentioned above are often cited as triggers.

What are the triggers for these Sentiments?

Stress triggers, anxiety notion, and the stress cycle that begin at one person and moving onto the following. In any case they can be classified into the likely triggers like,

Heartfelt connections

Connections can be a minefield of anticipated triggers that can cause tension, negativity and anxiety. However, if the couple is at the point of beginning their relationship, the excitement of being with another person can be overwhelming your psychological and health at home.

Disputs or disagreements between a partner could be a very unpleasant experience at any time within the marriage. If couples aren't effective communicaters, the absence of compromise among them could cause tensions.

Family Issues

It is impossible to choose your family In any case in the event that they make the feeling of being angry or sad, it's very difficult to eliminate the person from your life completely. Therefore, putting your energy into their presence could result in more stressed and have a greater number of negativity.

The birth of a child is typically among the biggest experiences a person is able to enjoy. While it's a thrilling experience but the new responsibilities it entails can become an issue for some people.

There are some who may be questioned about how they can be great guardians. Many are also stressed about the stress this could create for their profession as well as public activities and personal budgets.

Kinship

Like your intimate connections and friendships, your social circle could make you feel uneasy especially when you are unable to resist pointing out your fellows' mistakes. Additionally, you may begin holding on to negative thoughts about your friends in the event you do not speak with them. The worry about the outcome of your friendship with them is normal, especially when you begin to doubt yourself believing that you must keep in contact with them.

Professions as well as Profession

The current job or profession could cause you to feel these feelings especially when you dislike the work you do. Insisting yourself on working for an organization that is not really your passion could lead to the gruelling, dismal and unfulfilling life.

Cash

Financial concerns, such as the need to pay off obligations or setting money aside, generally affect those who feel the negative effects of these emotions. Surprised bills as well as a sudden increase in financial instability have also been recognized as points of strength many individuals.

Misfortune

The misfortunes of life are often accompanied by extreme feelings of bitterness or dread, as well as lament. Anyone who has recently experienced the loss of a loved one or family member may have an uneasy perspective on how their lives could be like from this point to. Additionally, they may have doubts regarding the circumstances which led to the unfortunate event. There are those who try to be particularly stressed out that they will not be able to recover from their pain and will never experience normality from here on out.

Injury

Personal injuries, regardless of whether physically, verbally, or sexual in nature, are stressful for anyone. Most of the time, they will do not last for long and are particularly so when the victim is unable to resist the urge to soothe that moment to his/her brain over and often.

Health problems

A sudden or alarming discovery, especially related to severe illnesses that are ongoing, can cause stress, negativity or anxiety.

Because it's a private matter and private, the consequences of receiving this information will be felt deeply by the individual.

Some people have multiple triggers for their anxiety, thoughts of negative stress, and anxiety. Certain individuals experience mental disruptions without a clear reason.

As a result it is important to evaluate your own behavior and identify what cause these thoughts to arise within your. This is why you'll need to be able to manage them more effectively in the future.

Note them down in a diary

One method that can help you determine the triggers that cause you stress is to start with a journal that's dedicated to logging your events and feelings associated with stress positive or negative thought, or anxiety.

It doesn't require an expert essayist to maintain journals. Whatever you are able to convey thoughts and feelings in a journal, it can make a powerful personal management device to use.

Avoid stressing over grammar rules or spelling. It is not necessary be confined to the socially acceptable or extremely delicate. The journal you keep is your own sanctuary and a place to discover the real you.

For you to guide you through the process to help you through this process, here are a few crucial hints you could use:

Find a place where you can write without getting distracted or interrupted.

Try to record on your journal something similar to every day at least.

When you are describing private injuries Try getting your thoughts concerning the incident, in contrast to the subtleties of the specific injuries.

You should take the time to reflect on what you've got in your mind on paper.

Keep your journal away from prying eyes by keeping it your diary in a safe place.

What are the reasons you should record Your Thoughts on Paper

In writing down your experiences as well as your thoughts in a journal You will likely to

You should give yourself more time to address them;

will be much more targeted when it comes to taking care of and evaluating individual concerns;

Increase your capacity to take on your stress triggers as well as other burdens that come with the day-to-day life;

transform your negativity into something that is more creative and open as well as

gain an understanding of the ways to move forward through these experiences and feelings.

A feeling of being uneasy or having a negative idea, or being worried is a normal part that make up human beings that are the same that they occur to you occasionally. If you're experiencing the same issues on a daily basis indicates that there is a deeper problems that are affecting all of us here.

If you believe that these thoughts are starting to impact the ethos of your daily life you should at this point you must decide on a way to admit your need for assistance. need help and you'll want to take action regarding this concern soon.

Study of a case

In the end, having decided to take a shot in reducing her tendency to overthink things, Millie decided that the most efficient method to start was to record her experience during the entire encounter. As a result Millie would be given the opportunity to look through her notes to contemplate the different approaches she could employ.

As Millie was able to discern and interpreted the problem the issue, all she had to decide now was determine what caused her to be a bit unsure. The rundown was divided into three parts: unease as well as negative reasons and stress. For each of them, she added the sub-categories that go with it such as family, companions and heartfelt connections as well as work, financial and well-being.

For more than 14 weeks, Millie recorded in the diary the thoughts and feelings she had regarding what triggers her thoughts. Millie took as long as was necessary to assign the appropriate classes to each of them.

After she had finished her rundown with her report, she went over it and realized that the majority of her triggers were associated. Three triggers from these frequently occurring topics came up. She was confident of being an educator was easily shaken by a comment by a friend. The teacher was anxious about any points guardians were positioned in front of her and inquire regarding the conduct in their children's studying hall. The upcoming presentation test about her also enraged her for a long time.

The Pareto 80/20 rulewhich states that the majority of her worries could be resolved through a gradual reduction of 20 percent of the concerns and Millie was able to assess the likely answers to her concerns about overthinking.

Tests for practice

Recall the list of questions you made in the exam for the previous portion. Much like the ones Millie identified, you can identify the triggers that caused your anxiety, the stressors and negative thoughts which caused you to think too much.

Use this table layout to record your reaction:

Feelings of unease   Negative thought Instresses

Close bond

Family-related issues

Kinship

Vocation and work

Cash

Misfortune

Injury

Wellbeing

In the next step, try to include regular subjects in your response. In order to maximize your efforts It is recommended to focus on settling a few problems that may affect your success.

Repeating Subject #1:
_____

Repetition Subject #2 Subject #2:
_____

Repetition of Subject #3:
_____

Section II

Techniques to Quit Over thinking

Chapter 12: Ending The Conflict And Welcoming Inspiration

Consider the Brilliant side of life.

This can be more difficult than you might think. With the way we live in, it's easy to make the positive aspects of our lives and make an idealistic approach with everything you do However, it can be difficult to finish this single exercise.

It could be due to many factors that stem from the fact it is a given that you'll be aware of something that is negative when you turn on the television to catch the news the early hours of the day. This is in addition or that your neighbour could irritate you enough that you may want to do an unjustified act. The unstable nature of our modern world is proving difficult for anyone to settle down on the possibility of being optimistic and have a jolly way to face life, and to stick to that decision.

Since it's essential for you to accomplish this, the following are the reasons to be adamant to think about your life's positive aspects everyday.

One thing you can see towards the positive aspect of life and your experiences will bring to you is that it can help you create a positive attitude towards others. This is known as having a positive mindset and is important to make progress. Research and analysis conducted through many years have shown that in order to achieve success is to take it as an the obligation to have a rethink of your perspective to the point that you develop a mind which is positive, and look across the globe from the perspective of a professional. That is what watching things from a positive perspective can bring about.

Instead of wailing about your experience of getting an answer from your boss at work You can use it as an the obligation to look at issues from the positive side. Being successful in the role that leaders use this approach will result in you changing the whole experience to sound similar to the way your boss phoned you to inform that tardiness is a characteristic. Also, you can decide to take on a task to observe a more impressive version of yourself pushing forward. It is a method of looking into it. If it is done in this manner you'll see you will have created the space to fulfill your career as well as to be more persuasive.

A look at the bright side of things will leave virtually nothing to be concerned about. When you experience the surge of positive energy that results from the shift in outlook it is likely that you are infused with energy that may be absent if that all you did was stare at your wall for the whole day, and be frustrated by events that been happening to you. Stress and anxiety can arise out of a variety of causes such as the fear of not having the power to manage your situation. However, once you begin to look at the positive aspects of life and see the positive side, you begin to perceive yourself in the light of someone with the power to control what happens. In turn, you'll notice that you start losing the stress associated with it, and instead the feeling of control will begin to emerge within you.

An investigation conducted by a team of experts and researchers revealed that an optimistic outlook towards your life can help you overcome chronic health problems of various varieties. Although it can be difficult to maintain an optimistic outlook to life after having have been taught about a imminent wellness issue, choosing to live from the perspective instead of looking at the bright aspect of life and having the confidence to face it to it can lead to the odds of being successful for the foreseeable future, seeming to never end, and will allow you to grow possibility of being more.

Instead of being the ones that float in despair your situation, you'll get more chances to become more productive and achieve more success when you are able to look at issues from the bright perspective.

After we've given an overview of all the benefits you will reap from exploring the positive aspect of life, the next few are useful tips to make sure you get this done.

Conduct a mental assessment of people within your everyday life, then focus on securing the balance. There are some people that you meet in your everyday life who are unable else to contribute other than their own harm. They come to you with only bad reports. They do not call whenever something exciting happens like getting married or receiving an upgrade. It is possible that they call you and get close to you when they've got horrible information to give. This type of person shouldn't be an essential element of your existence, because they'll make every effort you make to that fail to succeed in almost no time. As a result, you should create an emotional list of people who are part of your everyday living and then start to pick the ones that have created a responsibility that they don't see the value in you or don't give value on the daily activities you be a part of. Instead of allowing those people present in your everyday life (close to the negative power they have) make a commitment to get rid of them. They're just a source of food for your existence and the direction you'll end up, and it is a good idea to not bother about their burden into your life.

Be observant of your surroundings.

Take a look inwards. It is also one of the most important things to consider if you think that you are able to be positive in general. This is not sufficient for you to start taking people who aren't making a difference to your happiness from your existence. If you do not make a commitment to chip off your self make sure you are confident that everything will be fine for you. Explore your inner self and make a commitment to the most important points of your strength to make sure belief that, despite the events within you, you will not attain a stage that you're feeling so depressed and shattered. The first step is to identify yourself and your deep desire for a complete end to your existence.

Develop appreciation and practice it, making it a regular habit. It is among the secrets of successful people; they've practiced rehearsing appreciation as a part of their routine. It is a simple task, which requires paying attention to every positive thing that occurs for you regularly. When you're done observing the tiny nuances and God circumstances that occurred for you write them down in a journal. The training may be hard to follow at first However, the purpose is to help you reach an area where you can develop an eye trained to recognize the positive events and to feel happy in all circumstances.

When you're likely to be overcome by poor thoughts as well as the real nature of life that can be awful, try the great thoughts you are having. There has to be some silver lining that you can keep you afloat in every storm isn't it? This is the exact procedure you perform after you've finished this task. If you ever feel that you're likely to get overwhelmed with something that is negative choose one of your memories from quite long ago and put your attention on the memory. Make it an experience that brings smiles all over. This will make sure that you don't get overwhelmed by the feelings of failure which come with pondering antagonism continuously.

Talk to someone. Sometimes there will be times when it isn't straightforward to achieve without assistance from someone or anyone else. To this end, it is essential for you to talk with someone. You could talk to an expert or even a trusted person that can assist to get out of the bleak area, however the aim is to be sure you do not sink in the sea of feeling awful when you are able to contact someone who could provide help of some sort or other.

Take advantage of the present circumstances

In the past, we have pointed out the fact that one of the main reasons why some people never seem to be at a point where they can live up to their highest capabilities is because they spend excessive amounts of time being consumed by the past (which isn't something they can change) or thinking on the near future (which has yet to happen). This has the result that they never ever take a step back and embrace the present as well as should you aren't embracing the present and now, there is no chance of being anything great.

This is how objectively arranged people are able to determine if they can accomplish what they've set out to achieve, because they're worthy of it, and for others around them for the duration of their time. They are aware of this because they've been were worried about everything that was not happening, and had the choice to relax after some time realize that what they had accomplished was burning to the ground. Here are a few of arguments to show how you can take advantage of present circumstances.

Know this and be very clear on it. your past has been placed deliberately buried in the present. It is impossible to change it. the most effective method of looking into the past is to find a pattern that can be applied to the present and change your outlook for the future.

A man, for instance, who is recently feeling more fulfilled in his job could decide to live the life in which he was employed at his prior job. It is possible to choose to slack through the day and resent how he got dismissed, or decide to look into his dedication to this whole thing. Perhaps it was because the employee was not as effective as he could be, or there were a myriad of explanations as to the reason he felt more at ease. Instead of wailing endlessly over losing his job it is possible to offer to develop your skills to ensure to become an employable expert in the next company and thus be better equipped for his new role. This is the mindset one should adopt if you'll begin to accept your current circumstance.

Sometimes it is helpful to stop thinking about your main objective and focus on the small successes that can lead the goal. Let us be honest for a second; it's remarkable to experience a surge of dopamine and be thrilled by the fact of having a significant target to reach. However, it can seem overwhelming to just look at the goal. Therefore, instead of having a look at the main objective and becoming discouraged at how absurd it seems instead, focus on small wins that be the final goal. Instead of worrying about the distance you are from obtaining your Ph.D. is by all the accounts, concentrate on completing all of your classes on all of your exams and you'll be amazed at the speed at which you'll end reaching the ultimate target you've set you.

Understand that even the most impressive of plans aren't always secured. Another reason that you can't get everything done (as we've discussed before) is because you expend a great deal of time planning and laying down the steps to make what you want to happen for you. While it's important to follow a strict schedule however, you should keep in mind that even the most amazing and certain plans are in no way immune to the effects of certain unpredicted events. The information you read will help you think that the ideal option is live your life today and enjoy that the events unfold as they do. The things don't happen as you'd like them to so it's best you make this your priority when walking throughout your day.

Here are some suggestions of steps that can help in embracing what is happening right here and now.

Create your own drawn-out goals and then focus on winnings that are sporadic and will bring you to. Instead of looking at the vastness of your targets and thinking about the unimaginable aspect of it to you, break it down into distinct phases and pay attention to tiny progress. The multitude of actions put in place will result in an accomplishment of the goals that you set you.

Recognize that every second is a gift, and this isn't guaranteed. In this way, shouldn't use the gift that you've received on an unproductive task.

While it's good to let go of the past do not let go of your lessons learned through the years. They'll prove valuable to help you save time to come up with how you make decisions in the future. Find the drawings from earlier times and believe that they mattered to you because they have value.

Influence the Way You Think: Appreciation Vs. Lament Laments aren't widely used to serve at any level. They only detract from the current energy is required to make things happen independently. Instead of being disappointed and the data that stems from your way of thinking that you may have made improvements in the past, it is recommended to tackle this issue with a sense of gratitude.

Below are a few of easy things to take to move are moving from a place of frustration towards a place of gratitude.

Know the truth about the past. There is no one who sighs over things that were unfortunate for a people have experienced, but they do not know what happened to them. Instead of keeping the incidents that happened within your own life, feeling ashamed of them and not really transforming them look into your past to separate the events that have taken place in the past in the way they should be. You cannot alter the past. However, you could learn of it and carry on.

Concentrate on the gifts in everything. This can be difficult for you, especially if you're beginning intriguingly, however you need to be sure to not skip this step. Every time you've been through a tumult that you've experienced, there's the possibility of a reward. This may be a lesson you've discovered. Try to take this gift in and create an to fulfill your obligation of being grateful for the gift. Another way to convince that this is a part of your daily life is keeping an appreciation log. In this diary, you will record all of the events that has occurred to you and what you've discovered and encountered as a result of it. Create a habit of writing regularly, and you'll be amazed by the shift in brain it will bring you to.

Take action with certainty

It is the most important component of a successful person. If you believe that you are able to achieve anything remarkable or influence other people into having similar success for them then you consider starting with reducing the level of your confidence and turn into the person you wish to be seen as.

Usually, people who are in certainly throw the whole thing into the category of being rude. They are prone to dissociate themselves from everything happenings to them before conclude that the things they experience happen due to the fact that they're bashful people. If you look at the situation from this perspective the risk increases in the sense that you begin to leave the fate of a lot as well as sabotage the method you are able in transforming to be more successful.

If you've discovered that you're just not sure of what you wish to be, here are several techniques that will help you to reach your highest confidence degree. Here are some of the methods.

Be the first to be able to dominate something that is important today in the modern age. Most of the feelings of uncertainty as well as the tendency to hide from it, is due to the fact that you're not particularly good in a area. As an example, in the case that you were a highly skilled essayist, you would not be able to resist doing errands connected with writing every time an opportunity to write opens. If however, you weren't a great essayist, you'd turn down every opportunity to complete whatever is connected with the act of putting pen to paper. The same is true when you live your daily life. This could be your strength, ability or even the career path that you've picked. The goal is to make sure that you're so excellent at some area. This is the very first process to become confident of your abilities and what you could achieve.

Stop having that a lot of negative self-talk, and limiting issues to be aware of. One of the main reasons your struggle against your confidence level could be due to the fact that you're not constantly practicing to be able to hold a lot of conversations that aid you in remembering the extent to which you're afflicted throughout your daily life. If you let the voice in your head to jump at you as far as it can make sure the world know that you're inadequate, then exactly the same thing happens to you. your confidence will remain low in a way and not be able to do everything. Instead of having a lot of conversations with yourself that do nothing of value, can you begin by making positive assertions to reinforce your belief constantly until you discover how you can begin believing in the people around you?

Make sure you look like it. If you are able to perform and appear confident always you are at the point where it's up to you to establish a position where you are required to appear like you always. Adjust your posture; get rid of your slouched posture and keep your shoulders in place straighten up, stretch your chest and walk with your head up. If you're working wearing a suit, appear like someone you are. This will help in making sure that you're seen as confident, and you will begin to increase the level of confidence you have. People first notice you before anything else. Therefore, the necessity to alter your look.

Begin to surround yourself with people who know your worth, recognize your worth, and then move forward and show this to others. If you're looking to be certain, you will be part of the group of the dependable ones and be amazed at the things that will happen to you. However great you may be in something it will come to a point where you need to be comforted by a few people can help. In this case, being around them already will be beneficial for you.

Study of a case

In search of effective methods to combat the negative effects of anxiety and overthinking,

Millie coincidentally found the various exploration projects that were based on the subject that studies positive cognition. In the research, she realized that she was required to release the things that had happened to her in the past in order to open up for a positive future as well as the future. Also, she realized the fact that second thoughts over closed doors that were not opened to her time at university were preventing her from achieving.

In keeping these events in her diary Millie made a decision to implement some of the techniques she'd discovered about. At first she wrote a list of her endowments and the items she's grateful for in her daily life. She then duplicated every one in a new tacky way.

Because the majority of her triggers are business connected, she threw these notes the board that was next to her workplace. As such it was possible to without much of a hassle be able to see them any time she wanted to get a lift.

Over the course of seven weeks, she recorded the notes of what she was feeling after only a couple of minutes being at her desk. The notes she made were not significant, but regular alterations in her mental state, set in a step-by-step manner. One thing was certain: there was a variance however, it was, she allocated a space to look through a small portion of the notes she had posted.

She shared her views, Millie made plans to create a habit of remembering her blessings and assist her to recall what she was thankful for.

Practice Test

Create your gratitude list for people or things as well as life-changing events that you are thankful for in different aspects of your daily life. Utilize this design guideline in order to use this checklist to tackle questions that follow.

Heartfelt connection

Family

Kinship

Vocation and Work

Cash

Wellbeing

Other

As a result of your reaction Answer the following questions:

How do you feel when you hear this rerun?

What class or classes have the highest amount of records? Show your feelings about this particular aspect of your life.

Which classification/classes contains the most un-number of recorded things? Express the way you feel about this particular aspect of your life.

Are you better or a more shakier perspective in your daily day life? Why do you think that?

Chapter 13: Develop A Strategy For Your Day

The day's plan is among the most crucial, and difficult tasks on that can be accomplished with the help of a board tool accessible to anyone. In essence, a schedule for the day is a list of information on what you need to accomplish, the method by which you should finish it and the date it has to be done.

The principle behind making a schedule for a day is extremely fundamental. The concept has also been in use for quite a while. However however simple it might be, the difficulty of a program to follow is that most people ignore them eventually.

A few find it so fundamental that they feel it's ineffective at meeting the need. Many people are aware of the importance and advantages of a program to follow, but they fail to recognize how to keep it in place for long term.

In order to more effectively clarify to you the reasons you should make and follow a schedule for your day. The next section will discuss the consequences on your daily schedule if you don't have one within your daily routine.

What Would Your Life Be Like without a strategy for your day

It is turbulent in its own right. It is further complicated with the requirements and intricate details of modern-day methods to the everyday.

As you tackle the numerous tasks to be completed in a step-by-step manner, the pressure could quickly become overwhelming. As soon as the situation becomes overwhelming, the amount of anxiety you feel in your daily life can increase rapidly.

A lot of experts advocate the implementation of a schedule for each morning to handle your obligations and exercises more effectively. Yet, some individuals struggle to understand the plan right due to a tendency.

Focus on the fact that, there is no strategy to plan your day an individual's level of effectiveness will inevitably drop in. There are also these situations if you do not make a strategy for your day on your own

The process of jumping from one project before moving onto the next in effect, reducing the efficiency of completing your obligations;

not noticing significant cutoff times because you didn't remember that you had to do this in all cases;

Being defenseless to the interruptions that are likely to occur all around you.

In the effort of achieving harmony with your private lifestyle, work as well as your public activities and other activities;

You have no idea in any way specifically in regards to what you should immediately do; and not quite achieving the feeling of satisfaction when the day is over.

For determining these concerns You should attempt to organize your plan to your day based on your every day routine.

What is a plan for the day can help you avoid the tendency to think too much

One of the most detrimental results of excessive thinking is lack of motion. It means that you are caught in the process of contemplating the same issue repeatedly, with not having anything tangible to prove it. Then, at this moment, is passed on to you and you have no money for action or to complete various chores.

The plan you make for the day could assist in getting through this challenge by keeping you focussed and focused to the primary goal. In addition to improving your performance as well, it could help your mental health.

Based on research an effective plan for the day may include:

provide you with the energy to complete your work;

prevents you from getting distracted from your seemingly insignificant thoughts or other unnecessary elements from your present circumstances;

prevents you from performing boring ways to behave;

different confounded tasks which could cause feelings of tension and worry over not completing the stated goal;

You should work on your pace to reduce anxiety.

take away the stress to finish all tasks at once take away the pressure to complete everything at once

Let you be free of worry that you've failed to do something important.

In the end, having a plan for your day could also cause people to feel happy and content. An account of each of the items listed will serve as a confirmation that your day has proved highly beneficial. The goal is to avoid any feelings of anxiety, specifically ones of fear and self-esteem. Your psyche is likely to lack a good reason to continue a loop of unease or negative thoughts, as well as anxiety.

Make a plan for the day and adhere to it

People who can'tand aren't able tocreate a daily plan for their day think of the plan as weight. They see it as a checklist of things to be done and cutoff time to make. In the end, they are unable to regularly practicing creating and coping by a schedule for their day.

Certain people have a knack for maintaining a consistent and well-organized the right track. For those who haven't been designed or trained to perform this there are practical tips that can help you to stay on top of and stick to the plan to get through the day.

Begin your day with thoughtful considerations and thoughts.

It is the most important step you can take to organize a strategy to help you manage your daily routine successfully. Make sure you remember the advantages to keeping an organized list. Make a point of reliving how good you feel each time you can check items off your list. If you can do this, your brain will become accustomed to putting the things you want to do that day in order to make things happen, and you can check it off.

Setting a positive daily agenda

There is no way to instantly grasp the advantages of having an organized plan for your next day, but your upcoming self will see value of your efforts. No matter how good you can remember things your life could be a shock suddenly.

You may be left struggling to find your bearings and information. The day's plan that includes each of the crucial details that you need to keep in mind could make a huge difference during the tough times.

Place the things you have in your list, based on the importance of each item and personal preferences.

There are many who do not take advantage of the commonly used method for sorting out everything on their day-to-day plan. This is a crucial step to complete since it relies in your favor of finishing tasks. This way, you'll be able to focus on the work you have to do better.

A way to categorize your list is to organize your schedule according to the time it is required to be completed, as well as what you might want to complete should you're in a position to have more time. This way, you don't have to pass by the so-important cutoffs during your daily routine. Additionally, it will help to keep track of the tasks you could do in your spare time, keeping you from having to look around looking for something else to accomplish.

Be aware that your plans for the day can be subject to change.

Be aware that an agenda for your day is just a tool. Its elements are not decisions or requirements that you have to be following regardless of what. Sometimes, it is necessary alter the details on your list to meet your current requirements.

The idea of starting over is fine. It shows you're capable of adapting to any situations. When you figure out ways to alter your plans for the day You will be able to be able to better manage the stress and anxiety that sets off in at you from afar.

Make your plans for the day as a representation of the accomplishments you have made.

Making your way through your day requires the most investment and effort. Therefore, it's normal to be euphoric of completing your day's plan.

Instead of putting good feelings in the back of your mind, making it as a list of your accomplishments during the day can assist in adhering to this tendency.

It can also cause pondering to improve your mental health. Stress, anxiety as well as stress will take up virtually no place within your head after being filled with the accomplishments of your daytime.

Study of a case

Despite Millie's efforts to research expected methods but she felt that she wasn't making much progress regarding the subject. The main reason was due to the overwhelming amount of data that she had collected however, she wasn't confident about where she should begin. Also, she kept hopping around beginning with one method and moving to the next one, creating a pile of unfinished projects.

In order to determine this, Millie heeded the guidance from her most trusted friend and ken to create an outline of her plans for the day. As this was incredibly private the plan was downloaded as an errand executive application onto the phone so she is able to keep the plan of her day.

Millie also decided to write one summary for every common topic she'd identified previously. As such she'd be aware whether she'd performed something to address these problems. With the help of the software she set up the necessary level and scheduled regular updates to inform her periodically the actions she should take.

After seven consecutive days of following the daily plan, Millie at long last realized that she was back getting back into the flow and was able to complete her task.

overthinking.

Practice Test

Create your own agenda each day or as needed using the plan below. Be sure to adhere to the guidelines that are in the guidance on how to create a winning schedule that is effective.

To determine the "Need level" make sure that you assign every errand to a "high", "mid" or "low" score based on the overall level of desperation they show to you.

Use the "Status" segment on the next day to determine if you've completed your tasks.

Task# Task Status

You must complete the work on the spreadsheet you completed. The next day, you will be able to answer any questions based on the lessons you have learned:

Which number of assignments have you accomplished?

What did you feel like when you had completed your task?

How many errands have you never cultivated?

What do you think of yourself now that you didn't meet your goal from yesterday?

Do you know how to improve the level of your accomplishment?

Chapter 14: Keep Going With The Moderate Lifestyle

The process of learning to moderate is certain to alter your life if you know what it is and the best way to approach it. That's the truth and in certain cases the effectiveness of your efforts is hindered because you're still not able to master the process of taking the responsibility of your present situation both inwardly, sincerely physically, emotionally, and from every perspective. In this article we'll explore how to overcome this lack of power by focusing on the tasks that result from the manner that you're not yet able to control your environment.

The solution is exemplified in a one word: moderate. If you are able to grasp this concept and incorporate the knowledge into your daily life it will be evident that over the course of time the efficiency of your game will be at the next stage.

What is moderation?

Moderation is a design or form of workmanship that emphasizes a blatant simplicity. Actually, it is the practice of purposefully expanding the items we're consider most valuable and the deliberate removal of items which aren't as admired as we would like, or that keep us from making the most of those things that we are most grateful for.

The process of moderation revolves on the understanding of what is the most important thing that happens that you do, and it will bring about an observant ending of things that do not affect you in any way. When we talk about the concept of moderation, we must consider every aspect of your life, including the real home you buy and the right to be in your own space as well as the activities you dedicate you to do as well as the individuals who you let join your group and all the things of the other.

Minimalists (those who practice moderate living) believe that this mode lives is among the simplest ways to becoming extremely productive, loving and satisfied with your life, and playing your best every opportunity. It is based on the fact that no matter how much you don't have to be proud of your life, the items that you allow to remain within your personal, close to your home, and mental social space will forever affect how you reside and the way that you react to any circumstances that are thrown to you regularly. Someone who doesn't have as many dishes to wash in their home, has lesser dishes to clean when it is time to wash them, and thus has more time to concentrate on things that matter for him, when all is at stake.

When you begin to become more comfortable with moderation, keep in mind that cutting it back could be beneficial, but there are clear ways to ending this.

The advantages of living a moderate way of Life

A lot of people aren't embracing moderate behavior, mostly due to the fact that they're not yet able to appreciate the benefits that are available should they will adopt the idea of moderation in everyday daily life. In this section of the article we'll discuss the benefits of moderate living.

Moderating your behavior can assist in bringing an array of different things in perspective, as well as aiding you in making sense of what is important to you. As you're presently removing the chaos, as well as objects that do not seem to be a good fit having in your house are pushed to look at things from a larger perspective. you'll make basic options regarding what is to go and what remains. There is a good chance that you'll need all the food items at home, every one of clothing in the closet and all journals you keep on your table, and all of your devices that are stored in the shed until you realize that it is time to let some go. When you've made the option, and intend to keep everything until the last moment it will surprise you at what will be gone from your home by morning's conclusion.

Moderating your behavior can help in being focused and in control of your space. When you've begun to eliminate all of the chaos, you'll discover the feeling of "being in control" and it will start taking over you. It can be suffocating to find yourself within a space that's filled with a myriad of things and you may feel like that everything you see will be trying to keep your escape from this point.

When you are tempted to dismiss those feelings, just remember that it is time to begin making an effort to eliminate the mess. As you are beginning to out of your way it is when your sense of "being the one who is in charge" will be cultivated as well as your productivity increases close to the level of the time it.

Moderating your behavior can help to narrow down what really makes an impact on your life. As you've probably gathered here that the purpose of taking useless things off your home (truly mentally, spiritually as well as in general) to have only one reason: to help the mind to focus on things that affect you, and will have an impact over time. Once all has been cleared away then you're able to concentrate to the elements that are essential to your success.

Moderation increases the joy you feel. It is the result of being able to achieve the number of small wins that you'll experience as you work on your the art of moderation. As your effectiveness increases and you take control of the environment you're within, your energy levels increase with each additional thing you have studied before comes to pass eventually becoming a happier version of you.

Moderation will help you in bolstering your mind's self-view and a sense of certainty. Once you stop relying on the accumulation of properties, you'll be able to look towards the inside and bringing your focus to home lifting by looking from inside. It is one of the things that can result in a more positive perception of your identity.

Moderation will assist you achieve financial freedom. As you are more focused on getting and taking advantage of only those items that really make a significant difference for you and your family, the urge to stick to the extreme of monetary decisions, like excessive shopping, or the need to acquire things you don't need in the future could diminish.

Guidelines to Maintain an enlightened lifestyle We have emphasized how calming it down could be beneficial as far as moderate means - it's important to lay the foundation for a real. A quest for moderation shouldn't mean that you should gather all of the things you own and take your stuff out of the entrance. It is possible to manage this and should you decide to adopt an approach to living that is moderate and regardless of the consequences in a time-frame that is manageable and use the methods discussed in this section in the text.

The first step to moderation is an outlook. Whatever your intentions are looking to take everything you've got and then give it away at this moment, as long as you're not yet ready to make this that changes, you'll see immediately that everything you've handed out will be returned. Moderation's mindset is one that sees it as a necessary reference point, makes the case for itself, and then adjusts how anything isn't needed should to be kept away from it. It is this the place to get started on your journey towards moderation; it's also the point to change your perspective towards it.

Start by setting your goals clearly. You must be aware of the fact that, in this regard, there's no one-size-fits-all approach. There's not a general standard for the things you should have and what should not be in your possession. Moderation is a way of giving the user a set of rules to follow, and permits you to take the decisions with no assistance from others. There is no one to guide you and you'd have be able to establish CLEAR goals to you. What are the characteristics of moderation for you? Perhaps you need to clarify this first. You should also set a time limit for this project that you intend to quit.

Make sure you invest your money in products that are of the highest quality and extremely durable. The reason why you may own more than three items could be due to the basis that all of the three items isn't as good as the best high-end quality you can find. Are you able to allocate resources towards things which are better in quality and offer a wider range of functions than other items? Instead of having a printer as well as a scanner, the examining machine stacked on top of your office can you consider investing your resources towards purchasing one of the multi-purpose devices that include each of the three components?

Learn to live your life without a lot, avoid impulsive purchasing, and stick to the standard method of living with only those things that really have a positive impact on you. This is an early warning that it's usually the most difficult time when you're beginning the process that involves a continuation of living a more moderate lifestyle. As the years pass and you are conscious of the changes you've began, you'll see the improvement.

Take care to clean, please. The purpose of the exercise was to take those things not needed out of your home, and this is exactly what you should be making. That is the point where you begin investing the real effort in removing things of your existing situation. Make sure you are fair to your self as you go about this. What is it you're not using or no use to use? Please get these items out of your home. They could be given away or offer them for sale at an auction or whatever you want to do to do with these guys. Be aware that your goal is to have them leave your home following the period.

Utilize this similar cycle along with your own methods that you've employed when preparing your daily schedules. Keep this in the back of your mind Your daily schedule should include the tasks which are essential to accomplish this day. Do not jumble your agenda with tasks that ought not be in the first place. It could go against the the climactic, and result in lesser efficiency on your part.

Find out the value in recycling and reusing items, instead of buying new things just like clockwork. Reusing items is a great technique to prevent you from accumulating property again.

Find out how to improve your esteem by setting aside funds and putting it to other worthwhile endeavors. It's true, one of the main reasons to the reason you end up investing a significant amount for things do not really need is that you've got a lot of extra money after you have made all of your essential purchases. To make sure that you don't give in to the pressure caused by the fact that you have more cash than are able to handle make sure you check out reserve fund programs and explore the possibilities. In this way you will be required to understand the value of financial insight. It is a thing that can help you move forward with your day-to-day activities.

Study of a case

One strategy which Millie thought about was adopting a more moderate approach to of living. Before trying it out it was decided to explore first how she can apply it to essential areas in the day-to-day life of her. Given that the triggers she uses are related to business and business-related, she decided to narrow into that at this initial phase.

When she started her computer, Millie glanced through her files and emails to examine the current state of affairs. Her usual practice was to not have enough space to properly classify her documents into appropriate categories. A majority of them reside at her desk. In addition, her inbox was stuffed with messages that were not initiated from different places she had enrolled in as she led her exam.

In accordance with the guidelines of moderation Millie organized, deleted, and reorganized every single one of information and emails in the north, just outside of the multi-week. In addition, she removed herself from any newly joined email list that she no longer needed, which added to the flurry of mail of messages in her mailbox. When the process was over she experienced a sense of calm at the point she realized how organized her messages and files are.

To stay on top of things the woman included in her schedule to complete a regular cleaning of her files and her inbox.

Practice Test

Try to follow the guidelines mentioned earlier in order to reduce the amount of muddle in your advanced record. Try to save a backup of your messages and documents before continuing this task.

After you have completed this exercise, respond to the questions that follow in light of your experiences:

What would you think of yourself when you've completed the task?

Do you want to make a propensity from this? What is the difference? the way.

Chapter 15: Terribly Connections

Let go of your traumatic Memories

The process of letting go of the past isn't effortless or straightforward. However, we are all conditioned to hold onto things that are familiar and encouraging. If the underlying cause is something negative our psyches typically romanticize particular parts from the previous.

A few people blame their history as the reason behind the decisions they've made. As an example, Jake had a dreadful disagreement with his Secondary school friend, Beauty. Then, he decided to cut off all ties between Beauty and the other classmates at secondary school. He hoped that he would have recently gotten over the group in his existence.

The model shows how risky your past could be for your current as well as the future. What kind of memories you maintain influences the way you live your life and influences the course you will follow.

Then, in the unlikely occasion that you do keep a close eye on the past, specifically towards your bad experiences and experiences, you should be prepared for the possibility that despair and sadness will serve as your companions for the duration of your daily living.

If you want to shift your focus towards the most positive and rewarding in the near future, at this point, you have determine how you can let go of the previous mistakes. This is a must for all the mistakes you've made as well as the bad options that haunt your.

Past connections tend to be full of mishaps and bad decisions. They are however often the most difficult to let go of from long back. No matter how serious it was dealt with, people will always remember the experiences and feelings that they had with their former acquaintances.

To get rid of the recollections of your past, you have be proactive. The passage of time won't simply heal your injuries if you keep nagging at them. The goal is to discover ways of cutting off those ties that keep your back from letting go of the past, and moving on.

Being aware of the problem triggers the need for a response. The first thing you need to do is recognizing the true nature of an unhealthy relationship.

The Way to Identify an unfavorable relationship

A lot of people find it difficult to recognize whether they're in a bad relationship, or even otherwise. Certain people have been trained to recognize unhappiness in expressions of love as normal and others come up with excuses for the flaws of their partner. People who believe they're not doing enough within their relationship are frequently turn blind to the obvious signs in their surroundings.

A few issues with relationships could be disguised as basic characteristics you could identify ways to accept additional time. Whatever the case it is true that there are some important issues with relationships that may determine the fate of when a couple is in the middle of a relationship.

In order to help you discern warning signs that indicate a disastrous affair, here's a list of warning indications to be aware of:

It's like you want be able to transform yourself in order to comfortably match your companion.

It's totally acceptable to examine new hobbies you share with your spouse and see if you'd like to pursue these things. You can also modify your daily routine, in order to help support personal growth and development.

This can be a troublesome problem in the event that you believe the present version of you doesn't conform to the standards of your partner. If you change your style of dressing normally dress or, in the event that you change your perspective and opinions based on your companion's thoughts and opinions in that case it is at this point that your connection with them has gotten out of the realm beyond what's satisfactory and not.

It is important to protect your companion from relatives as well as your companions.

It is not necessary for everyone to be a fan of your partner It is a little disconcerting that none of the people you love most. If you notice that you're not happy with your relationships, it may be a sign that it is time to look into this.

Your spouse is constantly scolding your actions, at any time the fact that your analysis has been made public in a joking manner.

In doing so the accomplice has put yourself in a detachment powerful manner. Once you've had time, these feelings are likely to reduce your fear and can trigger feelings of anxiety in your body, thoughts of negative reflections, and worries about the outcome of your relationship with them.

It is common to think about what your companion is doing whenever you're away from him/her.

If your stomach has started to let you know something's wrong, it is best to begin by talking to your partner regarding your concerns and shortcomings. If they don't agree your opinion on this issue, in general it is because there's something else taking place that can significantly impact your relationship with them.

Being in a relationship of this type can be a bit tedious, particularly because it can cause people to overthink the things between the two of you.

The other person usually makes vast options for both of you without talking about it beforehand.

Review your relationship, assuming that you are the sole person making the major choices. The decision doesn't have to be nearly as significant as buying a house that is shared by both of you, without a discussion prior to the time. Participating in events by yourself the event he/she has to go to reflects the unbalanced overall effect of the two of you.

In certain instances, it's best to keep your distance from others for a short time, but your partner is not going to give you the space.

Self-care is essential whether or not you're dating somebody. The fact that you need to be alone does not mean that you are disapproving of the person you are with. In the event that the other person doesn't get it even after having explained your reasoning to the person, then you're at a point where the limits of your authority are not being respected. This is definitely not an ideal sign as it could lead to problems with control later.

You are obligated to the happiness of your partner.

If your partner is dependent on you alone and to feel content this could cause imbalance in your mental and emotional state. As an example, your companion blames you whenever they are angry or irritable. Additionally, the person is anticipating the need for you to correct whatever is going on or modify your behavior to make them feel better.

The situation could overwhelm the mind as well as your inner self. The feeling that you have to be careful around them in order to make them happy could indicate that you're engaged in a toxic relationship.

The person you are with controls or may will attempt to regulate your actions and the people you share your energy with.

A lot of relationship professionals see this to be the best advice be paying attention to. If you want to control your finances as well as your interactions with people and even your appearance, you must take an effort to distance yourself from the person. Analyze your relationship and let your personal interests be known in regards to the control issues he/she is imposing on you. What they say to you will determine if your relationship is worth being saved.

Inquire about whether you're engaged in a relationship that is not good for you.

The misunderstanding of the question could cause disappointment later. What you are pondering is that the fact that you're pondering this issue indicates that something is not right regarding your relationship to him or her.

Instead of pondering the responses to this query opting for a more active approach is the best. Engage with your co-worker to determine whether the relationship are able to be made better. If is not the case, then in that case, you should break off from the relationship prior to causing harm more.

While these indicators are designed primarily intended for people with close relationships, however many of these signs apply to all kinds of relationships exist in your daily everyday life. As an example, being dependent on a partner could be a burden on your well-being. An uncontrollable relative could also be just equally harmful to the one who controls your partner.

Examine all the connections you make in the day-to-day routine to determine if they are causing you to engage in excessive thinking, or make you feel anxious. If you've acknowledged that you have some issue, it is easier to find motivation to go on running your business and without these.

Confiscate Specific People

Once you have identified those connections that keep you from moving forward, you can start thinking about ways to let them go. In this way, you will create more room to happy people with similar views, beliefs as well as a similar outlook on life in the same way as you do.

You probably have some idea about the type of relationships you should make --

concerning the kind of people that you would like to meet or the traits you're looking for in your partner. Normally, you avoid people with a sense of discontent and interruption with their. If you're aiming to feel content and free from worries, then what is the reason you would choose to spend time with someone that causes you to be anxious?

The concept may seem obvious to you right now, but reality is that a lot of people fail to let go of these people in their day-to everyday lives. Uncertainties that one faces along with anxiety about becoming isolated during the course of daily life, could prevent the sound judgement from prevailing. Therefore, bad connections persist with pessimistic reflections as well as feelings one might experience.

Make sure you are aware of the people you surround yourself with, as they usually have more influence on your views and actions that you can imagine. Connect with those who are drawn to the beautiful things that happen in your daily existence, and not the individuals who prefer to stare and do nothing but sulk. Meet someone who is a fan of yours in the hope to have an admirable companion while you work towards achieving your goals.

Strategies to sever the most tainted Relationships in Your Life

In order to help you move in the direction that you've identified as dangerous Here are three crucial tips you could use to get rid of harmful people in your everyday life finally:

Establish and follow the limits you set.

Make clear the rules of the way you'll continue to work and impose them upon yourself. No matter how hard they try to break through the barriers that you've built within yourself, you must keep your feet on the ground no matter what.

In the event that you've let them be aware that you are shutting down any contact with them, refrain from answering their texts or calls. You can block them from your mobile and entertainment online accounts. Beware of being enticed to follow them because you've concluded that you're the moment done with these.

Do not be too accommodating to their wants and requirements.

The most harmful people will seek to take advantage of any affection or anxiety you feel in their interests. A good person may hinder your progress in moving on in the relationship.

There is no need to be a jerk toward them, however whatever. Don't try to aid them in their quest to gain a better perspective after the end of your relationship. It is not your responsibility to be responsible for your happiness.

Do not compromise your decision.

Be aware that the decision you made is based upon the many motivations you have to move with the relationship. If you find it difficult to remember the reasons, write them down on your calendar. So, you'll need to remind yourself of the reasons why you must remain steadfast in your decision, especially those you've eliminated of your life is attempting to come back.

Because of difficult relations, it isn't easy to cut off the connection. The only thing you have to do is to impose clear limitations regarding your future interactions with them.

I'd like to share an personal experience with this. There was a time when I shared a room with a person while I was engaged working 9-5 and was more an acquaintance than a companion. The two of us would have a great time doing work. In the middle of the night at the end of a pivotal work day, her behavior towards me changed. It's like she has did not know me, or that we never had a conversation.

www.ingramcontent.com/pod-product-compliance
Lightning Source LLC
Chambersburg PA
CBHW071445080526
44587CB00014B/1997